RAPE

"INITIAL SHOCK: THE BRIGITTE HARRIS STORY"

Based on a True Story

An Original Screen Play by Terri Johnson

Adapted Story by Olivia Shannon and Lamont Patterson

For information contact:
World Movement Publishing
409 N. Pacific Coast Highway, Suite 417
Redondo Beach, CA 90277
lamont@worldmovement.com or olivia@worldmovement.com
website: www.worldmovementpublishing.com

ISBN 10: 0982876831
ISBN 13: 978-0-9828768-3-1
Library of Congress Control Number 2015944072

World Movement Publishing books may be purchased for educational, business, or sales promotional use.
For information please contact:
World Movement Publishing
409 N. Pacific Coast Highway, Suite 417
Redondo Beach, CA 90277
lamont@worldmovement.com or olivia@worldmovement.com
website: www.worldmovementpublishing.com

This book is a work based on a true story. Some names, characters, places, and incidents have been changed to protect the innocent and any resemblance to actual persons, living or dead, businesses, companies, events or locales are entirely coincidental.

Cover design by Gabriel Ribot with DesignsBy-Gabriel.com AND Lamont Patterson with lamont@worldmovement.com

WORLD MOVEMENT PUBLISHING

ACKNOWLEDGMENTS

Thank you to the following individuals who without their contributions and support this book would not have been written:

BRIGITTE:
Marianne Bertuna, Attorney; Psychologists, Dawn Pallotta and Nicolleta Pallotta(manager of Women Against Violence Program in Brooklyn); Michael Cibella; Nancy Schaaff, Danita Giacomazza; Gloria Harmon; Rebecca Tubman; Laverne Chesson; Michael Ciebello; Arthur Aidala; Venita Arthur; Steps to End Family Violence; Women Against Violence Program;The Whole Defense Team including students at NYU Law School, all Psychologist, Dawn Hughes, Marianne Bertuna; In loving memory of Mother Mary Nerney 2014, founder of STEPS to End Family Violence

TERRI:
Sallie Elkordy; Oviawe Efosa George; All 400 Africans who wrote letters on behalf of Brigitte's freedom; William Scarboro; Cynthia McKinney; Arthur Aidala; Michael Cliebello; Steps to End Family Violence; Mother Mary, R.I.P. 2014; Governor Cuomo; Andrea Evans-Parole Board; Prison Guard who assisted with Brigitte's release; Jentry Johnson; Jonte Johnson; Freeman Bralock; Laura Mae Bralock; Carrie Ann Polk; Big Papa Lamont Patterson, Sr.; Lamont Patterson, Nichelle Patterson; Bruce Cecil; Stan Dorris; Olivia Shannon; Jan Honore; Lisa Thomas; Jacque Schauls; Bill Oxford; Michelle Carter; Skip Johnson; Tyron

Patterson; Gabriel Ribot; Deaundra Sheffield; Erica Sweeney; Zelda Johnson; Audry Ewells; Phyllis Kay Jones; Michael Blaylock; Kimberly Powell; Rose Belisle; Jerry Boyd; Lovelace Lee III; Latasha Holmes; Larry Holmes; Derek Rusel; In loving memory of Warner McGee-R.I.P. 2013

World Movement Publishing:
Terri Johnson, Brigitte Harris, Juanita Fussell, Sylvia Stokes, Margo Dill, Dr.Marian editors@firstediting.com, Nichelle Patterson, Andre Shannon, Gialani Shannon, Prophetess Lynnette Long, family and friends.

CHAPTER 1

As she sat near the window that burst with the sun's rays, her past haunted and invaded her mind. Suddenly, she snapped back to reality. Looking out the window, she soaked in the sun and the cool, calm breeze from the ocean as it flowed throughout her studio apartment she had rented in 2006, two blocks from the beach in Rockaway, Queens County, New York. Brigitte Harris loved this small community that attracted tourists during the summer to its sandy beaches. She wrote on MySpace about sweet beach parties, making s'mores, bonfires, getting drunk and watching the sun rise. It don't get no better than this, but she found she couldn't have a relationship. And, she was never able to go out with friends without getting drunk. Slowly, the front she'd created started coming apart. She tried to talk about the abuse with her family, but couldn't, and told many people she was a virgin. She had a mission to accomplish. Turning around and looking at her apartment, she admired how she had decorated the room with the pretty partition that separated her office from the living room, the couch with matching end tables, lamps and plants, and her small dining room set. Getting up, she walked towards her makeshift office with her desk and computer full of shiny new office supplies.

Sitting down in front of her computer, she surfed the web to research anything she could find on what preoccupied her mind. She found several articles and said, "He will be okay." Her mind told her that there would be no problems; and if there was a problem, it could be fixed. She let out a long sigh. Using Google, she searched for the object again and then placed her order via overnight delivery. *This is it and no turning back.* Staring at the computer, she let out another deep sigh. *Since no one else would stop you, I will.*

She got ready for work and put on her security uniform. While walking out the door, she thought, *I love my cousins. I've got to do something.* Feeling a heaviness in her soul, she needed to take some time off from work. *I'm going to request a two-week vacation. That's plenty of time.*

A FEW DAYS LATER

Scared and frantic, Brigitte washed blood off her hands while standing over the kitchen sink. She was careful not to let any drippings of blood touch her light-blue T-shirt, matching jeans, and light-blue chucks. She looked over her shoulder to see if the man, she had just bound and gagged was coming for her. She knew there was no way he could, but he had always haunted her. She scrubbed her hands, watching the blood run down the drain and careful not to let any get on her light-blue outfit. It always looked so nice next to her brown skin, and she wanted to wear it to work today. Drying her hands and throwing the paper towels in the trash, she suddenly smelled an awful stench in the air. Rushing back into the kitchen and holding her nose, she picked up the tongs and removed the flaming penis off the burner. Waving and patting the flames, she suddenly wrapped the penis in a dish rag and went into the living room looking down on the floor. The pretty partition was knocked down, lamps and end tables were scattered all over the floor, paper was strewn everywhere, tell-tale signs of a fight were everywhere. Breathing hard and panting she picked up the phone, dialed 911 and suddenly hung up. *I'm not calling the cops now, let me get out of here first.* Picking up her backpack, she threw scalpels, pepper spray, scissors, and pills into it. She hurried past the handcuffed and gagged man on the floor who was wearing rings, a watch, and a gold chain around an awful keloid neck. Disgust and hatred were her only thoughts.

Looking down at the man, she told him, "Bitch, you ain't never going to do anyone else like that again. You worthless piece of shit, and you gonna live the rest of your life just like that. Never again, motherfucker." And in a fit of rage, she screamed, "NEVER AGAIN," and began to cry.

Reaching past him, she grabbed her work jacket and ran towards the door onto the porch and sat down. After a short time Brigitte walked down the porch onto the sidewalk with the object wrapped in a rag. She saw her Spanish pregnant neighbor, Maria, and hid behind the shrub bush. Luckily, Maria didn't see Brigitte and got into her car and drove away. Crying hysterically, she let out a sigh of relief. Today was not the day to explain to a talkative neighbor as to why she was crying. *I'm glad she's gone.*

Scared, nervous, and checking over her shoulder, she walked down the street towards the police station. Everywhere it was noisy with cars, buses, people talking, music playing, and seagulls squawking. Looking around for a quiet spot next to a building, she pulled out her cell phone, covered her ear with her hand, and dialed the 911 operator.

"911 Operator."

Crying, Brigitte told the operator, "Someone is bleeding to death at 436 Beach 69th Street. Can you send an ambulance over?"

"What borough, ma'am?" the 911 operator asked.

"Queens," answered Brigitte.

"What is your name?" the operator asked again.

"Brigitte Harris," she said.

"Who is bleeding to death?" the 911 operator asked again.

"Walter Harris," responded Brigitte.

"Who is Walter Harris?" asked the 911 operator.

Looking around at the crowd, Brigitte told the operator, "He's my father."

Trying to obtain the facts, the 911 operator asked, "Why is he bleeding? What happened?"

There was silence. Brigitte refused to say anything.

"Are you hurt?" asked the 911 operator.

"No." responded Brigitte.

"Brigitte, what happened to Walter?" the 911 operator asked.

Silence again from Brigitte.

Brigitte sighed and said, "Forget it" and hung up the phone. She began to walk down the street toward the not-so-crowded boardwalk on the beach. She stumbled along wondering if Walter was still alive. What would the police find when they arrived? They'd find a man, bound and gagged, blood splattered on the wall, furniture upturned. But they wouldn't find her.

CHAPTER 2

S ounds of sirens were blazing and could be heard coming up to the address from two cops, two paramedics, and three firemen. Jumping out of their vehicles and running up to the porch, they noticed that the door was open. The policemen drew their guns and immediately called out, "NYDP, come out with your hands up." No one answered. The two policemen peered through the open door and scanned the area before entering the apartment. An odor hit them in the face. The apartment was in a mess with furniture lying on the floor, lamps broken, papers and office supplies strewn all over the floor. A little blood splatter could be seen on the wall and furniture. Finding a male body lying on the floor, bound and gagged, and no blood in site, they allowed the paramedics and firemen to enter the apartment.

Connie Davis, a black lady in her early 50s with a pulled-back ponytail and wearing workout gear was in the basement doing her daily workout listening to her music and panting as if she had a personal trainer. Suddenly, she heard her phone ring. It was her husband calling to tell her that the neighbors had called him and said that the police and everybody were at Brigitte's apartment. The neighbors wanted to know what was going on. Connie and her husband were the landlords and seldom have any police activity at their place. She replied, "Honey, I don't know. Let me go check it out." Connie raced upstairs onto the porch and saw that the police, paramedics, firemen, and a crowd of people had gathered in front of Brigitte's apartment.

Policeman Adams, nicknamed Red due to his curly red hair, hurried up the stairs with his partner, Policeman Franks, who was bald, following close behind him. After they had assessed the scene, and found a man bound and gagged, Adams asked, "Wasn't the initial call about someone bleeding to death? This man is not bleeding anywhere." He instructed Franks to go secure the front of the apartment with yellow tape as a crime scene. As Franks walked downstairs, he saw Connie and asked, "Are you the one who called the police?"

"No sir, but I'm the landlord here. My name is Connie Davis." As she wiped her forehead with a hand towel, Connie asked, "What's going on?"

"We got a call that someone was bleeding at this address," said Franks.

"What!!!" replied Connie as she tried to peek around Franks to see what was going on inside.

Franks took out a small notebook and pencil and started questioning Connie. "Do you know who lives here?"

"Brigitte Harris lives here. Is she okay? Is she in there?" Connie asked.

"No, she's not, and we need to talk to her. Okay, sorry, ma'am, can you please stand over here?" Pointing towards the walkway, holding the yellow roll of tape, and preparing to section off the crowd, he kinda helped her along with a little nudge in the small of her back. "I'll be back to ask you some questions," ordered Franks.

"No problem," said Connie.

Franks walked back upstairs to the apartment and, upon entering the room, he covered his nose with a handkerchief. "What the fuck is that smell?" He had smelled bad crime scenes before, but this was the worst. Firemen were standing with their glove-covered hands over their noses. Adams was looking around. He noticed blood splatter on the desk, wall and little drippings leading to the kitchen on the floor. Everyone had their hand over their noses.

Two paramedics—one a dark-haired Caucasian lady named Patty, and a very slim-to-skinny Caucasian male named Daniel—carried their medical kits and rolled a gurney towards the body. They knelt next to the body and prepared to examine the victim to see if he was still alive. Daniel reached for the man's wrist to feel for a pulse. There was none. "This man is dead," he said looking up at Adams and Franks. Daniel continued to look at the body, then slowly placed the dead man's arm on the floor. Adams was looking hard trying to find blood. He noticed a dark stain in the groin area of the victim. He asked one of the medics for a glove. Hastily, he put it on and swiped his hand over the stain, its blood. He took a pen from his suit-jacket pocket, and simultaneously lifted the waistline of the victim's pants and underwear. Suddenly, he jumped back and fell on the floor. He shouted, "Oh Fuck! His penis is gone!" Adams shouted, "Don't touch anything." He stood and stared at the body. His eyes slowly scanned the handcuffs on the deceased, the rag in his mouth, soiled stained pants, and no penis. *"This man was executed!"*

Franks told Adams that he ran into the landlord when he secured the scene and was going back outside to question her. Franks rushed out the door, down the stairs and flung his hand to get Connie's attention. She went under the tape, onto the porch, and crossed her arms as if she was running the show.

"Who did you say lives here, ma'am?" asked Franks.

"My friend, Brigitte Harris. Is she ok? Is she all right?" Connie asked.

"Did you hear or see her arguing or fighting with anyone?" Franks asked.

"No, I was working out in the basement, I couldn't hear anything," said Connie.

7

"What do you know about her? Can you give me any information? Did she live with a male companion?" asked Adams as he looked around at his surroundings.

"No, she stays by herself. She's quiet and stays to herself. I've only seen her with women. But she's a sweet girl. Is she ok?" asked Connie.

Franks was writing down everything she was saying trying not to miss any key points. The stench from the room had given him a slight headache. He started rubbing his eyes and head. He then heard his police radio squawk. He reached down to turn it off. "Well, she's not here, and we need to talk to her. Do you know where she could be or where she could have gone?" asked Franks.

"No, I don't know," said Connie.

"Have you ever had any problems with her as a tenant?" asked Franks.

"No, never, she is a sweet quite girl, never had any problems from her or her friends." Connie bit her lower lip nervously.

"Okay, ma'am, no more questions for now. Can you please step outside the tape for me? We will keep you posted as we know more," said Franks.

"Okay, just know I have rights, too, and I have a right know what's going on, sir. I'm not trying to give you a hard time, but please keep me informed, 'cause I still have to live here after all this is over and the cops go home," she said.

Franks was so tired of dealing with people like Connie. When would citizens just let him do his job?

As Franks walked back into Brigitte's apartment, he heard Adams calling Homicide and the Crime Lab. He looked towards the firemen and paramedics moving around the room and yelled, "Don't move. We are officially looking for this man's dick. Wouldn't want you to step on it. That is our evidence. It could be rolling around anywhere in this mess!"

Fireman Garcia looked ghastly as he stared at the floor and said, "Damn, I hope we find it." Other mouths dropped open in shock and everyone looked towards their feet, lifting them up off the floor as if they had already stepped on it. While almost throwing up, Paramedic Daniel said, "Man, this guy fucked up big time. Think he was cheating? Man, if he was, this adds a new twist to what happens when you get caught; and looking down at the dead man, he asked, "Is it worth it?"

Adams was beginning to get angry by the sarcastic remarks. He looked at the dead man and then at Daniel and said, "Well, I know what it's not worth. And that is you talking right about now. So, all of you stop fucking around. Get to work. We have a killer to catch."

Looking at Franks, Adams yelled, "Get that operator back on the phone now, and tell her to get that caller back on the line."

Sweating and shaking in her work jacket, Brigitte's heart beat fast as she walked swiftly towards the police department. She was scared and afraid of what was going to happen to her. Suddenly, her phone rang. With her heart racing fast enough to have a heart attack, she looked down at the phone and saw a private number. Reluctantly, she answered the phone. "Hello."

"Is this Brigitte Harris?" the caller asked.

Looking around she answered, "Yes."

"I am Detective Thompson. We received a call from you today regarding an incident that occurred in your apartment and we need you to come into the police station to ask you some questions."

Brigitte said, "Okay."

Thompson asked, "Where are you? I can send someone to pick you up."

"NO!" answered Brigitte.

"How soon can you get here?" Thompson asked.

She answered, "I am a block away." But Brigitte thought, *I don't want to go to jail.*

He responded, "Okay, we will be waiting for you." Thompson knew that you run for two reasons: either you are scared of something, or guilty. *Which one is she? I hope she comes in.*

After Brigitte hung up the phone, she didn't think she should walk into the police station. They were waiting for her. She knew they would arrest her once the questions started. *And, what do they know? No one helped me then so why would I think they would understand and help me now. I'm not going in there. I'm calling Debra.*

Just as Brigitte walked past the police station on her way to the pier, she bumped into Officer Samuels, a big, blond-haired, buffed cop coming out of the station wearing dark shades. Her heart dropped to the ground and beat so fast, she felt her heart beat to and fro. "I'm sorry, officer, I was just in a hurry."

Looking at her he said, "No problem. Slow down before you hurt someone."

She looked into his shades as she wiped sweat from her face using the same hand the penis was in. The reflection from his shades caused her to panic. She could see it was partially uncovered. How the cop did not see it, she did not know. She swiftly pulled down her hand and re-covered it inconspicuously. She then turned and walked away. Hoping he was not following, but too afraid to turn around and look. She headed to the Boardwalk Pier and immediately called her cousin.

On the other side of town, her cousin Debra Jones, dressed in a pair of tight jeans and a pink tank top, was in her bedroom sitting in front of her small mirrored table combing her afro hair. She had just bought a sterling silver afro pic and was trying it out on her hair. *"Yes, this will work".* Her phone rang. "Hello."

"Debra," said Brigitte.

"Hey girl, what's up?" Debra responded as she continued to look in the mirror patting her hair.

"Debra, I did a terrible thing," said Brigitte.

"What did you do? What happened?" answered Debra, now concerned.

As Debra listened to her younger cousin, her expression changed from happiness to astonishment, then shock and crying. "Oh GOD, what'd you do with it? Brigitte, do not turn yourself in yet. I'm coming. Where are you?"

"Outside the police station. The police called and want me to come in for questioning," stated Brigitte.

"What did you do with it? Wait for me. I'm coming. Don't go anywhere! Don't go into the police station. If you do, I'll never see you again. I'm going to get help. Just wait for me. I'm out the door. Meet me at the pier!" Debra said as she turned to look for her purse.

"Okay, I'll be at the Boardwalk somewhere. Just hurry up," answered Brigitte.

Grabbing her purse and keys, Debra ran out the door to meet her cousin.

Back at Brigitte's apartment, Homicide Detective Reynolds, a black male, nicely built, deep voice; and a white male, Homicide Detective Haskell, also well built in stature; and two crime lab techs; one Latino, Mario; and one black, Steve arrived to assess the situation.

"What're we dealing with?" Lieutenant Haskell asked. He looked like he had just gotten out of bed, with clothes wrinkly and shirt untucked.

Watching Haskell survey the room, Adams explained, "We have a deceased male, handcuffed, gagged, and castrated. Brigitte Harris lives here and her whereabouts are unknown. According to the landlady, the deceased does not live here."

Eyes scrolling down the man's body, Detective Reynolds, put on his gloves, squatted and examined the body. Looking at the blood around the body, he looked up toward the wall and desk and saw blood splatters. He asked, "So, whose blood is this? Maybe, it's blood from the person who handcuffed this guy." He looked up at Frank and told him, "Call the Coroner to get out here, NOW!" Looking towards the other officers, he told them to check the floors again everywhere. "Find that man's dick!"

While getting an evidence bag in which to place the bloody paper towels and gloves, Policeman Adams was near the stove and noticed that it was hot. He looked at the stove and saw an object that looked like meat on the burner. "Hey, Detective Reynolds, you might wanna come in here and take a look at this. I think we may have something here. Looks like burnt flesh and may be what we are smelling. The stove is hot."

Lab Tech Hanson followed Reynolds into the kitchen. Reynolds looked at the object and pulled out a bag and tweezers. He picked up the object and put it to his nose and realized this is where the stench was coming from. And, yes it could possibly be flesh.

Crime Lab Tec Hanson also walked towards the stove to look at the object and stated, "If I had to guess, I would say, yes. We'll know for sure when we run forensics."

Reynolds saw a computer in the living room and hastily walked over to it, went around the desk, and saw a blinking message. He hit the space bar and up popped a video dated July 25th three days prior to Walter's death. A dark-skinned slightly-thick girl with purple and blue hair was sitting in a chair. Suddenly, the girl in the chair spoke. "Okay, so testing right now. My name is Brigitte Harris, and this is the story of my life. Well, not the whole thing, obviously. It'll take way too long. Just the summary reasons: why I'm doing what I'm about to do, why I feel I have to do it, why it must be done, and why I've waited this long to do it. And so, you can judge me. But before you do, get the whole story. That's all I ask. Please get all the facts before you judge me."

Reynolds squinted his eyes and looked at the screen, "We need this computer, fingerprints and everything else lying around this computer. Check the bathroom for any signs of evidence. I don't care if there is piss and shit in that toilet, I want that too. I want everything that seems and looks suspicious!" shouted Reynolds as he continued to stare at the computer. While searching the area of the body, Crime Lab Tech Hanson, saw a scalpel picked it up and placed it in a bag. "What the hell did this guy do?" asked Hanson.

Back at the boardwalk, Brigitte cried as she walked along the railing. She knew people were staring at her, but she couldn't help it. She thought about committing suicide. *I hate him for what he did to me. I hate him so bad.* Brigitte looked at the hand that was still holding the object, stared at it and then threw it in the ocean. No regrets, no feelings, no sorrow, just good riddance and hatred for the owner of the object. A bench was a few feet behind her. Sitting down, she took out a scalpel slit both her wrists and pulled the sleeves down. Thinking to herself, *why could he not admit that he was wrong? Why did he try to do that to me again?*

Finally arriving at the pier, Debra drove up and stopped the car. Not even taking time to see if she was in the parking stall, she jumped out of the car and ran towards Brigitte. Brigitte saw her cousin and cried out, "I did it. I cut it off." Debra noticed that her cousin was in a daze and delusional. Debra asked, "Where is it?" as she grabbed the backpack thinking it was in there. Debra's mouth dropped open when she saw the scalpels, scissors and a bottle of sleeping pills. *"Sleeping pills?"* Debra checked out her cousin.

Brigitte met Debra's eyes, still crying. "I had to protect my cousins. I could not let him take them to Liberia and do the things he did to me. He had to be stopped."

"I know, Brigitte. I know." Debra wept with her cousin.

"He had to be stopped. I was not going to let him do to them what he did to me. I hate him for what he did to me."

Debra put her arm around Brigitte and tried to calm her down, but Brigitte continued with her confession, "I saw my cousin sitting on his lap, and all I could think of is that little girls do not sit on a man's knee and bounce around like that. They teach us not to be in a man's lap but turn away when it happens right in their faces. That man destroyed me. I'm not the only one he messed with. He hasn't changed." Debra reached for her cousin's hand and saw blood all over both her hands, wrist and now on her lap. She realized that Brigitte had cut her wrist. Debra took the rag that Brigitte had the object wrapped in and tried to wrap Brigitte's wrists and hold her.

"I love my cousins, and I would die for them, "Brigitte said crying on her cousin's shoulder.

"Oh my God, my God. Not today you're not. I'm getting you help," cried Debra. She pulled out her cell phone and called 911.

Five to ten minutes later, as Debra continued to comfort Brigitte and hold her wrists, sirens wailed up the boardwalk. Debra let go of her cousin to wave her arms and draw their attention. They arrived and got to work.

CHAPTER 3

CALIFORNIA

"Hey Grandma! Look, look!" Up in the sky was a pretty kite floating in the air. While running on the beach laughing and giggling, little four-year-old Jay Polk was full of excitement. This was his first time flying a kite and it was awesome. His kite suddenly flew up higher in the air and bobbed from side to side as the warm ocean breeze kept the kite adrift.

"Wow, you're flying that kite, and that kite is as big as you! But, you kept it going," said Terri Johnson, his grandmother.

Kneeling down, she grabbed her grandson and gave him a big hug and kiss. Jay was all smiles and very proud for what he had just done.

"Jay, it's getting late. Turn the spool of string and bring the kite down softly. You can do it."

"Okay, Grandma. That was fun," Jay, said smiling as he watched the kite float slowly down.

A few hours later, Terri gave Jay a bath. The scent of strawberry bubble bath floated in the air as she watched her grandson splash and play in the bathtub. She couldn't help thinking about her own terrible experiences of sexual abuse, and how she must protect her grandson at all costs. She knew that she needed to instill the teachings of what people should not be doing to him, period. Trying to figure out a pleasant way to spark up the conversation without causing him to look at her like she is an idiot, Terri hatched a plan on what to say and put it into action. She whispered to herself, "God please help me with this."

"Jay, Grandma loves you very much. And I was so happy to see you were flying that kite like the big boys. You are good. "Terri said as she smiled at her grandson.

"I know, Grandma. I'm good," Jay said as he splashed around in the tub.

"Yes, you are. I saw a man watching you fly that kite today. He had on a red baseball cap and a red jacket. Did you see him? Terri asked.

"No, grandma. I saw a lot of man's out there," responded Jay.

"Men not man's," Terri replied. "There are lots of bad people out in the world, and you must be very careful of your surroundings at all times," said Terri.

"Yes, Grandma," Jay said as he played with his boat.

"Is anyone doing bad things to you or touching you on your pee pee or heinie?" Terri asked as she looked her grandson in the face but pointed to his private area and his li'l heinie.

"No," he said, as his eyes bucked a little as if to ask, *"why would anyone do that to me?"*

"Always remember this. If someone touches you there, always tell, yell, tell," said Terri.

"Yes, Grandma," said Jay.

Terri pours a bag of alphabet toys into the bath tub and teaches him how to spell t-e-l-l, y-e-l-l, t-e-l-l-.

"See Grandma," Jay said as they spelled together in unison "t-e-l-l, y-e-l-l and t-e-l-l-."

CHAPTER 4

NEW YORK

Debra saw the medics jump out of the ambulance and rush over to Brigitte who, with wild electric blue hair, was crying, and despondent, sitting on the bench, with her wrists bleeding. They realized that she needed immediate assistance. They checked her fast-beating pulse, and her heart rate and unwrapped, then rewrapped her wrists. Brigitte was quiet, unresponsive, and in shock. Debra explained that she found her cousin that way. They assisted Brigitte onto the gurney and into the ambulance and rushed her to Staten Island Hospital.

Brigitte was extremely anxious and cried while the medics rushed her into the emergency room. While Debra provided information on her, the doctor listened and then proceeded to attend to her patient. Dr. Warner saw that both her wrists had been wrapped. She ordered the nurse to check the severity of the wounds, prep for possible blood transfusion, and then ordered a five-point suicide restraint to be administered. "I am Dr. Clarisse Warner. What is your name?"

"Brigitte Harris," she said looking dazed.

"Explain to me what happened," asked Dr. Warner.

Crying profusely Brigitte said, "I tried to stop him. I really, really tried to talk to him. He tried to do it again."

Dr. Warner looked at Debra who was also crying and worried. "Can you tell me what happened?"

JOHNSON, SHANNON, PATTERSON

"She said that she cut off our father's penis and wants to die. Then she tried to commit suicide. Can she be arrested?" Debra asked as she blurted out question after question while looking around at Brigitte.

"Due to her state of mind, she is a threat and a danger to herself and everyone else. She will not be released to them until they provide us with a warrant from the D.A. Her safety is at risk, and she needs to be observed and treated," said Dr. Warner.

"Dr. Warner, thank you so much. Would you tell her that I will be back with someone whose gonna help her? And, please don't let her kill herself," said Debra.

Dr. Warner explained, "No, not now. But our immediate focus of her assessment will be based on the safety of Brigitte and the level of observation necessary to maintain her safety. I won't pull the wool over your eyes, the cops will come. So, you have a little time. Maybe one week, maybe three weeks, but you need to get back here quick. I will call you if anything happens."

"Thank you so much." Dr. Warner grabbed Debra's arm, hugged her and gave her a look of hope. Debra left the hospital through the long corridor. Dr. Warner went back in the room to check on Brigitte who had several nurses at her side re-dressing the wounds and applying restraints.

"I don't want to be here and wished none of this had happened. Why are you restraining me? Don't put me in this. Just let me kill myself then you won't have to restrain me." She screamed at the top of her lungs. "Let me out," she said as she began tugging and moving trying to release herself but to no avail. "It was their fault, and I hate them all. All of them saw it. They knew what went on. They knew what he was going to do, but I'm the monster. What's going to happen to me now?" Brigitte yelled at the nurses like she was possessed in the Exorcist.

CHAPTER 5

CALIFORNIA

Diamond Smith, a sexy petite black girl, fair skinned and dressed in tight jeans and a cut up rhinestone t-shirt with bling, and bling jewelry was feeling good and thinking about nothing but having fun. Driving in her champagne-colored Cadillac truck with tinted windows and sitting on twenty rims with music blasting got off the freeway headed towards Long Beach where her best friend lived. Turning down her radio, she grabbed her cell phone.

Terri heard the phone ring. "Hello."

"Hey girlie, you almost ready? Just got off the freeway. I'm like ten minutes away," Diamond said as she bounced to the music.

"Yeah, my son picked up Jay about thirty minutes ago. Just doing my hair. Come on," Terri said.

"Okay, bye." Hanging up the phone, the music went back in blast mode.

Diamond continued to cruise through the streets of scenic Long Beach with its parks, sandy beaches and tropical trees until she reached Terri's golden stucco building with beautiful landscaping and beachfront apartments.

Hearing the music and a horn honking, Terri looked out the window and saw Diamond roll up to her apartment. Dressed in white legging tights with an orange pastel flared blouse with braids and hoop earrings, Terri grabbed her red skate bag and rushed out the door. Before hopping into the truck, she did a little dance, and they both laughed, sang, and high-fived while they listened to "Function at the Junction."

Fifteen minutes later, Terri and Diamond were sitting inside the skating rink with its flashing multi-color lights, gold carpet, wood floor, and jamming music from the DJ booth. Referees were ready and dressed in their black and white striped uniforms.

"What's up, ya'll? We rolling trio?" said Harold.

Diamond looked at Harold. "Ahrite."

"Fa'sho," said Terri.

And as the music began to play and disco lights flashed in rainbow colors, Terri and her friends began to skate and dance around the rink.

CHAPTER 6

Brigitte was heavily medicated, restrained and had lost touch with reality succumbing to a subliminal dreamy sleep of a gothic, Lady Vengeance, The original Dark Angel she always claimed to be. This was a female warrior with long blue wavy hair with a braided rope around her waist, a gold medal on her forehead with a light glowing halo above her head and a spear. She was standing tall as if she had just conquered the world.

Suddenly, Brigitte awakened to find that she was still in her restraint and tried to tug her way out. Nurse Betty Hampton, a 5foot, 9inch stockily-built Caucasian woman with gray hair walked into her room pushing a cart with her breakfast and meds.

"Good morning, Brigitte. The doctor wants to see you after breakfast. How are you feeling this morning?" asked Nurse Hampton.

"I'm feeling better. Can we take off these restraints?" asked Brigitte.

"Long as you behave, I can remove them so you can eat," said Nurse Hampton as she rolled the tray up to her bed.

"I will," said Brigitte.

" 'Cause if not, I will restrain you and feed you like a baby, and you don't want to make me have to do that, now do you?"

asked Nurse Hampton with a stern look like, *you don't want to go there with me,* and hands on her hips.

After removing the restraints, Brigitte scarfed down her breakfast while Nurse Hampton returned with a wheel chair to transport her to Dr. Warner's office, just down the hall. As they entered Dr. Warner's office, Nurse Hampton asked, "Is there anything else, Dr. Warner?"

"No, I think we'll be fine. I'll page you if I need you. Please close the door behind you,"

Looking around Dr. Warner's office, Brigitte saw a neatly-decorated room. She noticed several medical books lined up against the wall and plants placed randomly throughout. A photo on Dr. Warner's desk portraying her husband and son caught Brigitte's interest.

"How are you feeling?" asked Dr. Warner.

Brigitte responded with an "okay."

"I spoke with your cousin, Debra, and gathered some of your history. Since you seem to be doing a little better today, I'll make a change to your chart for 'no restraints.' I can't have you trying to kill yourself, so any outbursts, I will have to restrain you again. You do understand?" asked Dr. Warner.

"Yes, thank you, Doc. So, what are you gonna tell me? Am I crazy, insane, or possessed?" asked Brigitte.

As Dr. Warner watched Brigitte, she asked, "Which do you think you are?"

"Well, the average person would not be able to do what I did, so, I guess I'm insane. My father has been molesting and raping me since I was three." Brigitte's mind wondered off as she described what he did to her. Tears rolled down her face. "I couldn't let him take my cousins to Liberia. He would do to them what he did to me. And, I think he had already started. He had my cousin bouncing her on his knees. He was laughing, knowing what he was doing, stimulating her little clit and making her feel funny down there. Am I crazy, insane for what I did?" Brigitte asked as she stared back at Dr. Warner.

"I won't go so far as to say you are insane, or crazy, and you're surely not possessed. You are suffering from severe PTSD," said Dr. Warner.

Brigitte held her head down and said, "That sounds like all of them combined in one."

"No, PTSD means you are suffering from something that happened to you in your past. Many people suffer from this, and it can be stabilized. It stands for Post-Traumatic Stress Disorder. And along with PTSD, some people suffer from a dissociative disorder, in which a person becomes disconnected from their emotions or thoughts. This is common among sexual-abuse survivors whose memories of rape become overwhelming. Now, the fact that you saw the cycle about to repeat itself with your cousins does not help matters either. That really compounded the problem. Counseling and medication can help. And, from the story I've heard, you are going to need a lot of that, because your past is repeating itself, and you have become defensive about the issue."

With hatred in her eyes, Brigitte shouted, "I cut off his dick! I don't have to be defensive anymore and that weapon is gone for good."

Dr. Warner, not wanting to overwhelm her in one day, looked at Brigitte and asked her if she wanted to go back to her room.

Brigitte grabbed Dr. Warner's family picture and said, "I'm looking around your office and you have many awards. So I know you are a smart woman. But, let me ask you. Why will you listen and believe me?"

While taking notes, Dr. Warner told Brigitte, "I want to help you. Besides suffering from severe Post-Traumatic Stress Disorder, you also have a Personality Disorder."

"What is that?" asked Brigitte as she frowned and looked at Dr. Warner.

"You constantly have flashbacks and re-live the past. It can be stabilized with psychiatric help and medications," said Dr. Warner.

Brigitte looked back at the picture in her hand then suddenly asked, "What would you do if your son comes to you and says daddy is touching me. You're pretty smart with all these awards." While flinging her arms around, Brigitte asked again, "What would you do? Would you say, hey honey, let's go for counseling since you are molesting our son?" And, with a smirk on her face, "Or would you try to hurt him, or better yet, kill him, or tell your son he's lying about his dad? I mean, what is the logical thing to do in this situation? Huh? What would you have done?"

She put the picture in Dr. Warner's face and then slammed the picture on the desk. Brigitte smiled with a smirk on her face. Dr. Warner glared back at Brigitte with a look of concern.

All of a sudden without even a knock, the door swung open and in walked Nurse Hampton who looked quite agitated and out of breath. "Dr. Warner..." not realizing what had just happened in the doctor's office with Brigitte.

Brigitte looked at Nurse Hampton and said, "Don't panic. The doc is fine, and I'm sure she is done with me. Can I please go back to my room?"

Looking at Brigitte a bit confused at her statement and then back at Dr. Warner, Nurse Hampton said, "Dr. Warner, sorry to barge in like this, but the police are here looking for Brigitte to arrest her."

"Let me handle this. Take Brigitte back to her room and no restraints. Give her a sedative. I will talk to them," said Dr. Warner.

Dr. Warner walked out of her room into the corridor and saw two policemen.

She asked them, "May I help you?"

Officer Allen told her, "Ma'am we are here to pick up Brigitte Harris."

Dr. Warner made clear to them that she was not going to release Brigitte. "I'm sorry. Without a warrant she is not leaving

24

this hospital. I can't release Brigitte to you. So, you do need to leave."

Glaring at Dr. Warner, Officer Allen told her, "Since you know so much about the law, you are aware we have a legal right to stay here posted at her door to make sure she doesn't leave."

"Hey, do your job and I will do mine." Dr. Warner turned and left the corridor.

At that moment, Nurse Hampton knew they could not take Brigitte. She rolled her up to the cops and passed them going down the hallway.

CHAPTER 7

Swooping around hillside curves and down the streets, a white 750 BMW with shiny chrome rims, blasted beats from the radio. "I wish it would rain," could be heard from the driver as he sang along eventually making his way into a residential neighborhood and turning the car into a dimly-lit, curved back driveway that led up to a lavish home. He turned off the engine, stepped out of the car, and walked onto brick-encased tropical-fish-tank steps.

Attorney Jeffrey Michaels, a tall, debonair, and very handsome man fixed his tie and buttoned his navy-blue suit jacket. He rang the doorbell. Mrs. Gina Assante, an elegant woman with short tapered hair, wearing a beautiful sarong with African house sandals could be seen through the stained-glass front door.

Gina opened the door, "Hey, Jeff."

He replied, "Hello Gina, you are looking nice, as always."

"Thanks, Jeff. It's been a while since I've seen you. You've picked up a little weight, I see," said Gina.

He chuckled, "Yeah, just a tad bit. Where's the man of the hour? "

Gina tells him he's out back and Jeff heads towards that direction. With a look of slight desperation, he walked past her and told her, "Thank you." He continued to the well-landscaped, exotic, red-brick backyard. Two red haired Afghan dogs gazed at Jeffrey as he walked by the double doors leading into the bedroom.

Sitting in the Jacuzzi was Attorney Gorman Assante, a handsome, white, cigar-smoking man. Looking up, he saw Jeffrey. "Hey man, it's good to see you again. How you've been?"

"I'm good. I see you back here chillin' like you're a Tony Montana," Michaels laughed.

Pointing his finger at Jeffrey, Gorman told him, "You need people like me so you can point your fucking fingers and say, 'that's the bad guy.' Well, say goodnight to da bad guy. Sorry man, just joking. What's on your mind?"

"It is business, but on a personal level. Since you started me as an attorney, I highly value your expertise with complicated cases. My dear friend has a cousin who is in serious trouble. Her name is Brigitte Harris, and she is being charged with second degree murder, and first degree manslaughter of her father. Her story is horrible," said Jeffrey.

"Think it could be self-defense?" Gorman asked as he rubbed his hands together.

"At this point, I'm not clear on the particulars. Don't know if he attacked her, or if she just out-right killed him. And right now, she is at the Staten Island psych ward under suicide watch. They have not arrested her yet. And, the police are waiting on a warrant from the District Attorney. From the information given by Debra, Brigitte tried to prevent her father from taking her little cousins to Liberia," Jeffrey said.

"I'm sure there is more to this story. Do you know the accused?" asked Gorman.

"I've never met Brigitte, but based on my friendship with Debra, I want to help, despite the circumstances," Jeffrey said.

As he looked up at Jeffrey, Gorman said, "Okay, I need to meet with her. I will decide at that time what we are up against defense-wise."

JOHNSON, SHANNON, PATTERSON

Offering drinks to both attorneys at the poolside, Mrs. Assante looked at her husband, "Honey, let me freshen up your drink. Would you like a drink, Jeff?"

"Yes, I'll take a scotch, if you have it."

"Glen Fiddich, of course," said Mrs. Assante.

Gorman watched his wife as she walked back into the home to prepare the drinks. He then turned towards Jeffrey waiting to hear more of the story.

"Thanks dear," said Gorman to his wife.

"So, this is a situation where I will need your expertise. She needs the best, and you are it," Jeff said with desperation in his voice.

Getting out of the Jacuzzi, Gorman grabbed his towel and wrapped it around his lower body. He grabbed his cigar, re-lit it, puffed on it, and got himself ready to hear the rest of the story.

Gina returned and handed her husband and Jeff their drinks. Before leaving, she kissed her husband on the cheek, rubbed his backside, and then returned to the house. Gorman takes a sip and looked at his friend and asked, "What did she do?"

Jeffrey speaks nervously, "Take another drink and grab your dick, because his was cut, burnt, and thrown in the ocean. She castrated him by overpowering him with pepper spray; stuffed his mouth with a towel, and then wrapped duct tape around his mouth and neck," said Jeffrey.

Gorman opened his mouth in shock, "Get the fuck out! Whattt!"

"I've seen you in action at your defense trials, and I know that you are the best. I've seen you. Please, man, I know it sounds barbaric, but something really bad had to happen to this girl for her to do something like this. She experienced something real bad, and I mean *bad* to want to go that far. You represented that blue-eyed butcher who stabbed her husband over 193 times for the drug-induced physical and mental abuse that he inflicted upon her. You got her twenty years as opposed to the death penalty—the best defense I have ever seen in a court room. Man, you know you're good."

"Tell you what. I'll talk to her on your behalf, ASAP. I need to hear the full story from her and see the autopsy results," Gorman said as he watched his friend. He knew this meant a lot to him. "Thanks, I told Debra I would put you in contact with her. Here is Debra's phone number and the name of the doctor at Staten Island Hospital who is treating Brigitte. Her name is Dr. Clarisse Warner," said Jeffrey. He gave the written information to Gorman.

"Thanks. I'll get on it right away. Now, I'm going to cut this short. Don't mean to be rude, but I have a massage in thirty minutes," said Gorman.

"No problem, man, I can let myself out. I'm the one who came unannounced," replied Jeff. He reached out to shake Gorman's hand and turned and headed towards the house to leave. Gina raised her voice a little to tell Jeff to let her walk him out and he does.

CHAPTER 8

LOS ANGELES

Leaving the skating rink, Terri decided to leave with Andre Franklin and got into his car. Contemplating where they will get something to eat, they decide to go to the local hamburger stand and get some pastramis. They pulled into the driveway and parked, got out of the car and walked up to the window.

Looking up at the menu, Terri stated what she wanted. "Um, I want a pastrami, fries, and a coke. All of a sudden she heard pop, pop, pop, pop, sounds like firecrackers. As she turned around, she saw a young teenage boy, around fifteen year old, light-skinned, saggy clothes, cornrows, and drug-induced glassy eyes, as if he had smoked a pound of angel dust, holding a nine millimeter. They made eye contact and the young boy suddenly pointed the gun at her and pulled the trigger. It jammed. He pulled it again and then suddenly BANG. A blast of fire burst from the gun. The bullet flew through the air as if in slow motion and smoke sizzled.

"Get yo ass down, girl!! Don't you hear those damn gun-shots? That muther fucker shooting at us. Get down," shouted Andre.

He yanked Terri to the ground and checked to see if she had been shot. Blood shot out of her body and spread all over her blouse. Diamond, who met them there, was scared, tears streamed down her face as she tried to call 911. Andre was calling Terri's name and began to panic. Two thugs were waiting in a burgundy low-rider Impala car with the engine running, waiting to take off. The shooter ran and jumped into the car. The car screeched out of sight. Innocent bystanders who had fallen on the ground, looked all around and checked to make sure it was safe to get up. Andre looked at Terri and did not see where she had been shot. Not wanting to wait on the paramedics, he carried her to his car and rushed off to the hospital.

"I've been shot! What the fuck! I been shot. Man, I can't believe this shit. I'm shot. I'm gonna die. My kids. Don't let ...," and suddenly she drifted off and passed out.

Speeding towards the hospital, Andre saw that Terri had slumped over. He reached over to touch her pulse and felt the beat of her heart. "Don't die on me, Terri!" and drove up to the hospital emergency door honking his horn and waiting on the staff to rush out.

"Terri, don't you die on me!"

CHAPTER 9

NEW YORK

Sitting in their high tech office, reviewing notes and wanted pictures plastered on the walls, the two detectives reviewed all the evidence.

"Wow, we have a full confession," voiced Reynolds as he sipped on coffee and ate a doughnut.

"And, we have the murder weapon," said Haskell.

"What we got on fingerprints?" asked Reynolds.

Flipping through the report, Haskell said, "We have fingerprints from the kitchen and on the scalpel."

Walking over to Reynold's desk, Haskell hit the computer keys and brought up Brigitte's picture, the look of sweetness and innocence. She was standing next to a tree, wearing a green and white seersucker short set. This photo did not match the crime.

"Just wanted to put the face to the crime. I'm looking at her picture and thinking about the crime—they just do not match. You thinking what I am thinking?" asked Haskell.

"Man, just keeping it real, I don't even know. I mean, I don't know what I'm thinking," stated Reynolds. But, deep down inside, he was thinking. *What led her to commit such a crime as this?*

CHAPTER 10

Nurse Hampton and two other nurses were working at their nurse's station behind the lighted intake counter in the main reception area. The double doors to the hospital reception area suddenly opened. Debra walked into the hospital as straight as she could, dressed in a floral sun dress, high heels, afro puff, and feeling confident to have Attorney Assante, dressed in a grey and burgundy pinstriped suit at her side. She knew the nurses were watching them walk down the hall. He was the kind of man that drew attention from everyone.

Nurse Hampton looked at both of them and asked, "May I help you?"

And, then, looking at Debra, "Oh, I remember you. You are Brigitte's cousin."

"Hi, my name is Gorman Assante. I am here to see Brigitte Harris. I have been hired as her attorney. I understand that she is on suicide watch. Will I be able to see her? If not, I will need to speak with her doctor. Is she in?"

"Yes, the doctor is expecting us," said Debra.

Nurse Hampton made a phone call. "Sorry to disturb you again, Doctor, but Brigitte's cousin is back, and she has an attorney with her. They are requesting to see Brigitte."

Nurse Hampton hung up the phone and within a few minutes, Doctor Warner came down the corridor towards them.

33

"Hi, I'm Dr. Warner." She stuck out her hand and shook Assante's hand.

"I am Attorney, Gorman Assante, and we are here to see Brigitte Harris."

"Brigitte is fine. She has been given a mild sedative, and the suicide restraints have been removed. I think she may be coherent enough to talk to you. Follow me."

As they entered her room, they saw her lying in a slightly upright position in her bed. Her electric blue hair was all over her head, and bandages could be seen on both of her wrists. Debra picked up her wrists and looked at them. Brigitte expressed a look of relief.

Assante strolled up to the bed and placed a gentle hand on Brigitte's arm. She looked up at him with some alarm. "Hello, Brigitte. How are you? I'm Gorman Assante. I am an attorney here in New York. I was referred by your cousin's friend, Jeffrey Michaels."

Debra told Brigitte, "I've told him what happened, but he needs to hear from you. You can trust him. Tell him everything."

Brigitte looked at Assante and then towards her cousin. "Okay, can I have a glass of water? My mouth is a little dry from all of these meds."

Doctor Warner nodded her head and gave orders to her nurse to bring her some water. Assante then pulled up a chair next to her bed and took out a yellow pad and pen from his briefcase. Debra walked to the side of Brigitte's bed as Dr. Warner stood at the foot of the bed.

Assante cleared his throat. "Brigitte, if I am going to defend you, I need you to tell me everything. I need all the facts."

The nurse came in with Brigitte's water and placed the pitcher and a cup on her bedside tray. After pouring a cup, Brigitte took a sip looking at Assante.

"Brigitte, you can trust me. I'm on your side. I'm here to help you, not hurt you, and I surely won't judge you," assured Assante.

Debra walked on the side of Brigitte's bed and pulled out a comb from her purse and proceeded to comb Brigitte's hair. Brigitte wanted reassurance. "I want Dr. Warner to stay here with me. Is that okay?"

"Yes, I actually think it's a good idea for you to stay, Dr. Warner," Assante said.

Brigitte looked towards Dr. Warner. "Dr. Warner, I want to apologize for the way I acted with you on my last visit. I just wanted you to know that what happened to me can happen to anyone. I'm just like you. A good person. I'm a good person, but I wanted you to know that what happened to me could happen to you or anyone."

Dr. Warner smiled and nodded her head. "I already know, Brigitte."

Brigitte then turned towards Attorney Assante and began to tell her story.

CHAPTER 11

With a look of disgust, lust, and perversion, he sat on the bed with a blanket thrown over his shoulder. I was three years old. He was twenty-nine years old. And, as young as I was, I remember exactly what he and I were both wearing. He wore black pants and a black sweater. I wore a multi-printed dress and matching panties with shiny shoes that were patent leather, and my hair was combed with pretty braids. He suddenly picked me up and placed me on his knees. He began to bounce me on his knees. Up and down, up and down. His hold was not right, and I wanted to get down.

"Daddy, I don't wanna ride any more. I don't wanna ride no rollercoaster anymore. Stop, Daddy. Stop!" I cried.

"Okay baby, you must be tired. Wanna lie down?" asked Walter.

"No, I don't wanna lay down. I want to go outside and play with the other kids. Why they not in here playing this game?" cried Brigitte.

And in a whispering voice, he said, "They can play, too, but Daddy wants to play with you first. Daddy wants to play."

"What game?" I asked.

"Daddy loves you, and this is the way all daddies show love for their little girls," said Walter.

Walter began to hug and hold her. His hands began to run up and down her tiny, small body while lying her down on the bed. Brigitte knew this was not right and began to cry. He suddenly began to unzip his pants. She remembers him getting on top of her and trying to have sex with her. She remembered the phone rang and pleaded with her father to go answer the phone and him telling her, "Don't worry about it."

She remembered him getting off her in time. She remembered grabbing her doll. And her brothers peered through the door snickering because they thought she was being punished for being bad. She remembered being in pain. She was three years old. Brigitte was about four when her father first forced her to perform oral sex on him. "He sat on the bed and he took his pants off, pulled his penis out, and told me to suck on it, "she remembered later. " And I guess I was doing it wrong, so he said, 'Suck on it like a bottle.' And, I guess I still wasn't doing it the right way because he laughed and said, 'Don't worry. I'll teach you.' "

"No, Daddy. No, Daddy, stop," I pleaded.

"Shhhh, Daddy loves you. Shhhhh, it's all right. I love you baby. Relax."

"This was the beginning of years of rapes from my father," stated Brigitte.

CHAPTER 12

THE YEAR 1987

"I am six years old and was taken to live with my grand-mother, Grandma Hanna. Her house looked so nice and pretty from the outside. It was antique green with a very large porch and could have used a little paint. The yard was well kept and had a white picket fence around the yard. Kids were playing outside with a ball, laughing and having so much fun. I met my cousins, ten-year-old Bruce Watkins, twelve-year-old Carlton Sheppard and nine-year-old Debra Jones. And, for the very first time, I met my grandmother."

"My grandmother was a mean cruel woman who ruled her household with an iron fist. She showed favoritism and was very hateful. She did not have an ounce of love in her body," Brigitte said looking around with teary eyes. The memories were painful and she often wondered why her grandmother showed no love or affections for her. "We were treated as slaves, and as if we had to pay for being there."

CHAPTER 13

"After a year had gone by, I remember after attending church, I was in the bathroom changing my clothes into some pretty purple shorts, a white tank top and purple tennis shoes. And as I opened the door to go out, I was pushed quickly back into the bathroom by my cousin Bruce. He was dressed in a blue hoodie and jeans. He unzipped his pants and grabbed me by my head and forcibly pushed my head towards the opening of his pants. He told me that I had better not tell anyone and threatened me."

"'Get yo ass in here, and suck my dick,' Bruce said. "You gonna suck my dick. You know you want it, and if you don't, I am going to get you in so much trouble with Grandma. Grandma will make you stay with me, and I will make you do this every day. If you tell anyone, I will bring all my friends over here to fuck the shit out of you. And all at one time. And I better not feel your damn teeth or I am gonna knock you out."

"I try to pull away but he is holding me tighter and pushing my head down harder. I was so scared, and tears were falling from my eyes. Mama, Mama, help me. He ejaculates all in my mouth. Does anyone even notice the change in me?"

Brigitte took another drink of water and paused. Assante took her hand and Debra came closer.

"It is okay, Brigitte," he said. "Take all the time you need."

"I will continue," she said. "I just want to get the story out."

With teary eyes, she continued, "And just when you think things couldn't get any worse.

Debra forgot to flush the toilet. I got blamed for it. I remember getting up early in the morning and going to the bathroom to brush my teeth. I did not notice that someone had gone in there and had shit and left the shit floating in the toilet. I finished brushing my teeth and walked out of the bathroom and then all hell broke loose. My grandmother went into the bathroom behind me and then suddenly rushed out and came up to me. She snatched me very hard by the collar of my pink flannel pajamas and yanked all the clothes off of me. I was terrorized, scared and crying. I didn't even know what I did. Looking at me with such hatred in her eyes she said to me, "You shitted in that toilet and didn't even flush that toilet. I'm going to teach you a lesson, and I bet the next time you take a shit, you gonna flush that toilet. Don't nobody want to look at your shit!"

"She made my cousins watch and no one spoke up. My grandmother took a stick and beat me so hard that my skin split and was bruised. I remember screaming so hard from the pain. It was unbearable. She beat me till she got tired and was breathing hard. She then went in the kitchen and came back with a can of cayenne pepper. My Grandmother made me bend over and she poured that red pepper in my butt hole and then all over my body and making sure it covered every split of skin and bruise on my body. I cried and tried to tell her that I didn't do it, I didn't do it. I never could understand why she and the whole family was so mean and cruel."

"The last act of vengeance from my grandmother, I can't remember what I did at that time."

"One day, I was playing with my dolls, and my Grandmother comes to the hallway bedroom door and screams out my name. I remember jumping and turning around. Suddenly she threw with all her might a phone that hit me in my mouth and broke my front tooth. I don't even remember what I did for my

Grandmother to do that to me. When I saw my dad, I told him I fell down. I was too scared and had no reason to tell the truth. Why tell the truth when you already know that he was going to believe his mean-ass mother. She would have beaten me with a stick as she always did every chance she got."

Tears streamed down Brigitte's face as she described some of the incidents of her childhood. Debra cried too as she combed her cousin's hair. Brigitte stated her grandmother treated her as if she was her slave and her grandmother was the slave master. She had to do all the housework, cleaning and everything that her grandmother ordered. She was nothing to her grandmother and felt no love, only hate.

Dr. Warner came over to the bed and held Brigitte's hand. Assante reached out for her other hand in shock from what he was hearing.

"Are you okay? Can you go on, or do you want to stop?" asked Assante.

"No, I wanna talk, now that I have someone who will listen. You guys are listening to me. Finally, someone is listening to me," stated Brigitte.

"Okay, so at this point, did you tell your grandmother about what your cousin and father did to you?" asked Assante.

"No, she would not believe me, anyway. Besides, she loved my dad, and that was his mom, and he was her heart. My grandmother did not work, and he took care of her, making sure she had everything she needed. The Harris family is a different culture. In Africa, everything like Skeletons have to stay in the closet. 'Don't put your business out there.' They knew what he did. They just, for some reason, decided to protect him. Possibly because he was the bread-winner of the family, and if something happened to him, the family would be poor. So, they turned a blind eye for wealth and greed.

I did tell my mother. So she went to her pastor and told him, a Pentecostal pastor in Monrovia who lived in Shelia's building. He asked my mother why she was going through all she was going through...why I wasn't living with my father, or why he was not supporting us. My mother told him that I was being molested by my father and appealed to him for help. The pastor said he would confront Walter about the problem. But Walter conveniently made himself unavailable due to his busy business schedule. And the pastor made himself conveniently unavailable due to his busy church duties. This was a slap in my face and especially coming from the so-called "man of God." No one would help us, but people were aware of the rapes and abuse that occurred in that war-torn country. The pastor said he believed the story of abuse, but did nothing about it. "Whenever a war takes place, a lot of things happen. A lot of people become so evil and negatively inspired," Pastor said. "There have been a lot of rape cases around, but nothing was done about it, and they sided with him," said Brigitte."

"So, besides the beatings and rapes, was there anything else you had to endure?" asked Assante.

"I hope you don't turn against me for what I did. I could only imagine what your INITIAL SHOCK was when you first heard my story. I was trying to protect my cousins. I am not a murderer. His dying was an accident, and I did not intend to kill him. I put that rag in his mouth to shut him up. When I called 911, I thought he was alive and breathing. I really wanted to kill myself. I wanted him to walk around as a eunuch for the rest of his life, and the pepper spray was to blind him to keep him from looking at little girls. He needed to know that I was not playing, and he was not going to abuse my cousins or any other little girl. I wanted to kill myself instead of him. I know I will be punished. I tried to commit suicide, but I have a will to live now, and I don't want to get the death penalty. Will I get that?" asked Brigitte.

"No. It won't come to that. Please don't try anymore suicide attempts. It will be an honor to represent you. You will have a chance to go before the jury and tell your story. And, they will be the ones to judge you. It's better to be judged by twelve than to be carried out by six any day. I don't want you to worry about anything. Brigitte, I sincerely believe you," said Assante.

Brigitte sighed heavily. "Thank you so much, but I have no money to pay you."

He reassure Brigitte, "It would be an honor to represent you, pro bono."

"No one has ever believed me when I tried to tell them. Thank you," said Brigitte.

"Don't worry about anything. Get plenty of rest and get well. The District Attorney will issue a warrant for your arrest, but don't worry or panic. It is procedure with a crime of this magnitude. They will come for you. Do not discuss anything with them. Tell them you have an attorney and any questions they can contact me. I will call you tomorrow," Assante said.

CHAPTER 14

After talking to Assante, Brigitte was taken back to her hospital room, where she went and stood in front of a mirror. She saw her hair was combed into a cute hairdo and stared in amazement. She saw that she was beautiful, and no longer needed to hide in pain and shame. She could finally look at herself without crying or feeling ashamed.

After three weeks in the psyche ward, the warrant was issued, and Brigitte was arrested. Fully dressed in jeans, blue t-shirt and a wind breaker jacket, her blue hair was all over her head now, 250 pounds. She was handcuffed, walking through the hallway and looking around for help. The police escorted her out and put her into the squad car. As Dr. Warner was running out towards her, Officer Sanders stopped and warned her. "Please, doctor, step back. This young lady is going to be taken to jail. And, this time we have a warrant." Officer Sanders handed her the warrant and pushed her away from Brigitte. Dr. Warner read the warrant. "Nurse Hampton go inside and get Debra on the phone! Tell her they are taking Brigitte to jail. They have a warrant."

RIKER ISLAND JAIL - NIGHT

"Okay, give me your left hand. Now the right. Go stand in front of the wall facing the camera. Stand to the right and to the left. Now, turn around and face the camera. Go to the next

44

room and get your clothes. Your number is 347812," said the jail processor.

They took her to another room where she got undressed, bent over and had her vagina and rectum checked. She showered and got into the infamous orange jumpsuit.

As Brigitte was escorted to her cell, one guard reached out to personally shake Brigitte's hand and nodded her head in support of her, despite her charge. She was a rape victim herself. Brigitte looked all around, sat on the bed and grabbed her pillow. She used the toilet, removed her glasses, and pulled the covers back on the bed. Suddenly there was a loud noise, CLANK, and the switch turned off the lights. Pitch darkness. *"I'm scared to death. This is all my father's and grandmother's fault. They were supposed to protect me. Instead they abused me. This did not need to happen. Oh God, please help me."* Eventually, she fell asleep.

NEW YORK – COURTROOM

A few days later, Brigitte was standing next to Assante during the arraignment; the judge read the charges. "Brigitte Harris, you are charged with second degree murder and first degree manslaughter. You will be held without bail." And then suddenly, BAM! He slammed the gavel down as if he was breaking a piece of rock. The proceedings were closed. Expecting the charges that were read, Brigitte stood looking stone-faced and walked away slowly thinking, *I hate them!*

LOS ANGELES

Terri had been admitted in the emergency room, and Andre was by her side. Dr. Hill walked in. "I have some bad news. This hospital has been closed for five years, and this is the first day of its re-opening. We have no surgeon on staff who can handle a gunshot wound," said Dr. Hill.

"What the fuck? So you gonna let her die? Can't you do something? Why you open if you can't help anyone? Man, please, please you got to help her," said Andre.

Dr. Hill opened Terri's bloody blouse to check the wound. A nurse placed an IV in her arm and prepped her to take vital signs. Dr. Hill examined the wound and saw that the bullet went straight through. In and out. Dr. Hill told Andre that Terri will be taken to surgery to close up the wound. He called Dr. Sean Wyatt for assistance and ordered the nurses to move Terri to the operating room. X-rays were immediately taken and revealed the damage. As Terri was wheeled down the hall through the double doors to the surgery room, Dr. Hill went out to talk to Andre.

"Okay, it's a clean shot. It went in and out. We won't have to try to remove a bullet. That's what I was afraid of. So, with that being said, it is still serious. I've called Dr. Wyatt who will assist me. She is being prepped right now for surgery to close her up. Andre, the x-rays show that the bullet missed her heart by two inches, and she has internal bleeding. Dr. Wyatt and I are going to perform the surgery and stop the bleeding. We are going to do everything we can to save her life. Can you please wait in the waiting room? We will come get you as soon as we are done," said Dr. Hill.

"Please, just save her," pleaded Andre.

CHAPTER 15

NEW YORK – YEAR 2009

Two rugged female jail guards handcuffed and escorted Brigitte to the courtroom. Their footsteps echoed in slow motion, as they walked down the gloomy court hallway with only a little ray of light coming from the window behind them. She was wearing the jail house clothes of a blue suit and blue loafers. Her hair had been shaved. And, as she walked down that hallway wearing glasses, she held her head up high. She was seated next to Assante.

The courtroom was packed, standing room only with spectators and the media. The sheriff, bailiff, and courtroom stenographer were in position. The prosecuting and defending attorneys were seated and the jurors anxiously awaited the trial to begin. Tyson Harris, Sheena Harris, Dr. Warner and Aunt Glo were sitting behind Brigitte. Her cousin, Debra, was not there.

The bailiff finally made the announcement. "All Rise. Queens Court for the 11th Judicial District is in session. The Honorable Judge Hamilton presiding. All having business before this honorable court draw near, give attention, and you shall be heard."

Judge Hamilton made his announcement. "Have a seat Ladies and Gentlemen. This is case number 347812. People of the State of New York vs. Brigitte Harris. Everyone has been sworn in."

Looking at the jurors consisting of seven men and five women, Judge Hamilton explained the following instructions to them. "I'm admonishing you to decide this case only on the evidence lawfully presented in the courtroom. You must not conduct your own investigations, experiments, or research into the facts or law. You must follow the law contained in my instructions. Wait until all the evidence has been presented, and the case is submitted to you for group deliberation to determine guilt or innocence. Do you, and each of you, understand and agree that you will and truly will try this case now pending before this court and a true verdict is rendered according only to the evidence presented to you?"

"Yes, Your Honor," the jurors said in unison.

And looking towards the prosecuting attorneys, he asked, "Are the people ready to give their opening statements?"

"Yes, Your Honor," said Attorney Julia Hayes.

The prosecuting attorney, Julia Hayes, was dressed in a nice olive green suit and pumps. She stood before the jury very confident as her past trials spoke for themselves. She had won the majority of her cases, and the state wanted the best. She saw Walter's family members, Aunt Cora, and a couple of disgruntled family members, seated behind the prosecutor's side of the room.

Standing before the mixed jurors, she began her opening statements.

"Thank you, Your Honor. May it please the court, ladies and gentlemen of the jury, on behalf of the State of New York, I would like to thank you for your willingness to serve here today. Given the opportunity to hear the evidence that comes in, so that you can understand what has transpired. This is a very serious case, from acts of vengeful rage to brutal mutilation. Please listen carefully. You have the most important role in this matter. And that is determining whether the defendant is innocent or guilty. You will need to focus on the evidence concerning her mental state of mind. When she did what she did, was it a culpable state, meaning, did she know what she was doing? Or was this an act of wickedness to human life or depravity of mind?

48

This case may make you feel uneasy. Some testimonies will be graphic. The prosecution will present evidence proving beyond any reasonable doubt that she committed this crime out of vengeance, and she should be convicted of first degree intentional murder. Evidence will show, that he was pepper sprayed, handcuffed, gagged, and bound, then mutilated. In layman's terms, his penis was cut off with a scalpel. All the evidence is here to put her away for life. We have a full video confession and the murder weapon. We need a guilty verdict."

And then, Attorney Assante rose from his chair and looked into the eyes of every juror. "Thank you, your Honor. Ladies and gentlemen of the jury, I will present a case proving that Brigitte Harris suffered severe abuse, mental, physical and sexual abuse for years from her father, and that she was protecting not only herself, but her cousins. She is not guilty of murder. Her motive was not revenge. She was trying to prevent the cycle from repeating itself again. Her father intended to take her cousins to Liberia and molest them. You will see my client's intent was to do what no one else was willing to do, including what clergy, police, and family wouldn't do." Attorney Assante then turned around and walked back to his seat.

Watching Ms. Hayes stand up, Brigitte heard the bailiff say, "All witnesses have been sworn in, and Ms. Hayes, you may present your first witness."

"Thank you, Your Honor. Good morning, ladies and gentlemen. I call Mr. Komo Oviawe."

Mr. Oviawe, a Liberian official, was dressed in red and gold African attire and had an air of arrogance as he walked towards the witness stand.

Brigitte recognized Oviawe as one of her father's associates. She never liked him and knew that his labor force was young children. *Now what is she going to ask him? All he is going to do is lie with a straight face.*

"Mr. Oviawe, how are you?" asked Ms. Hayes.

"Fine, thank you," said Oviawe.

"The relevance of your testimony today is to tell the court what type of person you knew the victim to be. Please tell the court how you knew the victim," said Ms. Hayes.

Oviawe replied, "Walter and I worked together years ago in import and export of coffee in Liberia at Camwood. I later was promoted to another company and left. I lost contact with him after that. He later reached out to me through a mutual friend and wanted to know if I wanted to take a position at his new business venture of exporting and importing rubber. He also invited me to his boat party."

"So, would you say you had a good personal relationship with him outside of business dealings? Had you ever met his family?" asked Ms. Hayes.

Attorney Assante suddenly shouted, "Objection, Your Honor. The prosecution is asking a compound question."

Judge Hamilton sustained.

Ms. Hayes responded, "I'll rephrase the question, Your Honor. Did you have a personal relationship with Walter and his family?"

"No, I met his wife a couple of times. He spoke of his kids. We hung out a little, but we never got into each other's personal lives. We were more on a business level," replied Oviawe.

"Okay, let's get back to this party. You accepted the invite, so please tell the court what transpired between the two of you that night," stated Ms. Hayes.

Oviawe replied, "Yes, I accepted. It was a lavish event on a yacht with very important business people in attendance. We talked about work, and I offered him a position with my company. But he refused."

CHAPTER 16

It was a warm tropical night in Liberia, and the yacht was filled with party goers sailing into the night. Everyone was networking, mingling, and having a good time at the party of the century. Women were wearing beautiful African attire and evening gowns. The men wore Kofi hats, Dashikis and black-tie suits. Mr. Oviawe and his business partner, Shalama Uma, were talking to Walter and Xyere Tuga.

"Congratulations, Walter, I'm proud of you and your business success," said Oviawe.

"Thanks, I wanted you to share in my new-found business-venture extravaganza." Walter held up his drink for a toast and the others followed. "And to you, my friend, congratulations on your success in the diamond trade. Let me introduce you to Xyere."

Xyere Tuga was not his wife, but a dark-skinned model, a sculptured body with beauty and grace. Sitting there drinking and eating hors d' oeuvres, she sat up under Walter as if they were lovers. They were smiling at each other and whispering in each other's ears.

Xyere smiled. "Nice to meet you, Mr. Oviawe."

"You also." And still looking at Xyere but talking to Walter, "She's gorgeous, Walter."

"Thank you, my brotha," Walter said with a smile.

"And to you, congratulations in the rubber trade. You can make a lot of money there, but you can make triple more in the diamond trade. Why don't you come work for me? How about it, my friend?" asked Oviawe as he sipped on a drink.

"It's a wonderful offer, Komo, but I'm the boss for a change. I'm officially hiring people to work for me now. I do realize the money that can be made, but for now, I'm good," replied Walter.

"You know you always have an open opportunity with me. Don't hesitate to call me if you change your mind. Don't forget the fringe benefits," Oviawe said as he looked strangely at Walter.

Walter was looking around at the party, people dancing and drinking. Suddenly, he grabbed Xyere's hand, "Ok, will do, my friend. Now it's time to party. No more business talk." And they danced the night away.

CHAPTER 17

Hayes believed she had shown Walter's character as a decent business man, and not that of a child molester. She looked towards Judge Hamilton. "I'm finished with this witness, Your Honor."

Looking at Assante, Judge Hamilton asked, "Would you like to cross-examine this witness?"

Defense Attorney Assante dressed in a black suit, white shirt, yellow tie and looking very sharp responded, "Yes, Your Honor."

He walked up to the witness stand and asked, "So, Mr. Oviawe is it?"

"Yes," said Oviawe.

"You say you weren't pals with Walter, but you were at his party. Correct?" asked Assante.

"Yes, it wasn't' because we were pals. It was business," stated Oviawe.

"That's right, and you are in the business of importing and exporting diamonds, correct?" asked Assante.

"Yes, sir," Oviawe said as he glared at Assante.

"Would these be Blood Diamonds, where the diggers, I mean kids, are forced into labor to dig and dig for the jewels while experiencing brutality, ritual executions, and rapes as a weapon to control and terrorize them? And abductions of thousands of kids who are drugged and taught to kill and to protect these goods?" asked Assante as he glared back at Oviawe.

Mr. Oviawe fidgeted on the stand.

Attorney Hayes stood to her feet. "Objection, Your Honor. Defense is badgering the witness."

"Sustained. Where are you going with this counsel?" asked Judge Hamilton.

"Your Honor, these questions are relevant to this case. It's foundational in showing Walter's sexual desire for little girls since the late 70s while knowing the defendant."

Mr. Oviawe still fidgeted and squirmed in his seat. "This witness knew Walter liked young girls and knew he could use him in disciplinary acts toward little girls who did not want to obey. That's why he wanted Walter to work for him. This shows his pedophilic behavior did not start with his own child, but with other little innocent girls as well. He was a sick man. Spineless. Now, there's a word."

"Be careful. Proceed," warned Judge Hamilton.

"I just have one more question, Your Honor."

And looking towards Mr. Oviawe, Assante asked, "Isn't the reason you asked him to work for you is because you supplied him with nine young girls in the past for sexual favors, and he owed you a favor, to help rape young girls for slave labor of diamonds?"

"No, no way. I know nothing of this thing," Oviawe said as he looked nervously at Assante.

Attorney Hayes stood up. "Your Honor..."

Attorney Assante threw his hands up in the air. "I'm done with this witness." And walked away.

CHAPTER 18

Terri was at home recovering from her surgery. While she and Andre played backgammon, she reflected on her decorations: purple and turquoise color scheme with marble tables. Should she redecorate? It's a miracle she's alive. Maybe it's also time for a new look!

Watching Andre, she told him, "You always cheat when I'm winning. Why is that? Oh snaps, here we go."

Studying the backgammon board, Andre said, "I'm not cheating, and it's not my ego. It's strategy. Fuck all that. What did the D.A. say? Didn't you talk to him today?"

"He asked me how I was doing and informed me that they had not caught the shooter. He asked me a few more questions. Then told me it was probably a gang initiation and that drive by shootings have occurred numerous times at that hamburger stand before." Terri said while watching Andre make a move on the backgammon board.

Angry and upset, Andre replied, "Of course, it's in the hood. That's why they aren't doing anything about it."

As she shook the dice, threw them on the board and studied her moves, she told Andre, "Yep, you're right. He did say that I could get some money from the Victims of Crime. They will continue to look. And, I told him I will, too. . . Not."

55

"Yeah, right, if I see him, I'm going to bust a cap in his ass. He did a down low," said Andre. Thoughts of revenge crossed his mind, *I want to get that guy real bad.*

"I know the Terminator," Terri said smiling at Andre.

"Exterminator...No baby really, all jokes aside. I am glad you're alive. I wouldn't want nothing to happen to you," said Andre.

Terri looking at him and stated, "Thank you, baby. I know God spared my life for a reason. A purpose—and I need to find out why." Andre moved closer to Terri and kissed her.

NEW YORK

After listening to Dr. Warner's testimony regarding Brigitte's state of mind when she entered the hospital and her diagnosis, Assante asked her to step down. He then called Brigitte to the stand. Everyone was quiet and looked in awe, and were shocked that she was even taking the stand. Dr. Warner, Nurse Hampton, Connie, the medics, paramedics, homicide, cops, pregnant neighbor, and the 911 operator were in the courtroom. Other onlookers were anxiously waiting to hear her testimony.

Looking at Brigitte, Assante said, "Good morning. Please state your name for the record."

Noticing the quietness in the court room, she stated her name. "Brigitte Harris."

"And how did you know the deceased?" asked Assante.

With bitterness Brigitte said, "He was my father."

Assante asked her, "Biological or adopted?"

"Biological," she said with no affections in her voice.

"Okay, well, Brigitte I know in your heart you want to tell your story, and the reason you ended up here today. So, take a deep breath and tell us what happened," commanded Assante.

"Okay, it all started when...," and Brigitte began to tell her story.

CHAPTER 19

Brigitte was ironing her airport security uniform for work when the phone rang. It was her cousin, Debra. "Hello."

"Hey, Brig, Aunt Cora wants to invite you over for a family dinner. Walter will be there, and he wants to make amends for some of the dysfunction in the family. He says you won't take his calls, and he really wants to see you."

"No, I haven't taken his calls. All he wants is sex from me, and that's not going down." Brigitte said a little agitated.

"He just wants to say he's sorry. That's it. That's all," said Debra.

"Yeah, right, we'll see. I'll come. I have some things to say myself. This may be a good thing. When is it?" asked Brigitte.

"Sunday at noon. We're having a barbeque. Can you bring some potato salad?" asked Debra.

Brigitte said, "Yes, I can."

Happy to hear her cousin's response, Debra said, "Okay, I'll see you Sunday."

"Ok, bye." As she hung up the phone, Brigitte thought, *What is he up to?* She did not have a good feeling about this family dinner.

Everyone had gathered in the backyard under the shady trees of Aunt Cora's upscale country-style home. It was a very hot, humid day, and the music was playing loud getting everyone in a partying mood. The cook had the barbeque pit blazing and smelling good with Texas style ribs, chicken, and links. There was a tree bearing apples, and a tree house where children played jacks and marbles. The adults played dominoes and cards and could be heard talking loudly. Some girls were playing double-Dutch except for one little girl, Kayla. Kayla was sitting on Walter's lap. Brigitte walked up, greeted and hugged Aunt Cora. She handed her the potato salad.

"Hi, baby. Glad you could come by. I'm not in the best of health and don't get out much. Come by and see me some time. I'd love that," Aunt Cora told Brigitte.

"Ok, I will Auntie. The house was nice and the flowers were beautiful. Where's the...." Brigitte looked over and saw Walter was bouncing Kayla on his knee. Brigitte suddenly froze and became furious. She found Debra and pulled her into the house, trying not to make a scene. Brigitte confronted Debra about Walter and Kayla on his knee. Aunt Cora hearing the commotion, came into the kitchen to calm Brigitte down. Brigitte was so furious that she became combative with Debra and Aunt Cora.

"Debra, have you lost your fucking mind? Why is Kayla on his lap?" asked Brigitte.

"Why you tripping? They just playing. Calm your ass down," said Debra.

"Calm my ass down? I told you what he did to me and other girls, and you let him bounce her like that?" Brigitte said.

"Brigitte, honey what's wrong? Debra what's going on?" asked Aunt Cora.

Before Debra could answer, Walter took Kayla off his knee and burst in the kitchen with a surprised look on his face.

"What the hell is Kayla doing on your lap?" asked Brigitte.

"Just talking to Kayla about going to Liberia to see her homeland. I tried to call and tell you," said Walter.

"What!!! You taking her to Liberia! When?" shouted Brigitte.

"Around Thanksgiving time, and I am taking Dena, too," stated Walter.

"Brigitte, it's not often kids get a chance like this to go to another continent, especially to see their homeland. What's the problem? You went there," said Aunt Cora.

"Exactly." Brigitte said as she folded her arms.

Facing Aunt Cora, Brigitte tells her, "Debra, the mother of these girls, knows why I'm acting this way. Since you keep turning a blind eye to his sickness, it just shows me all the things you taught me mean nothing. I realize it's all about money in this damn family."

Aunt Cora was appalled at Brigitte's behavior, and the boldness of her conversation. Walking up to Brigitte, she told her, "Look, young lady, don't you dare talk to me like that in my house and with that tone in your voice."

Debra tells Brigitte, "Stop! Don't talk to Aunt Cora like that!"

Brigitte stepped back from Aunt Cora and told her, "You're right. This is your house. I mean no disrespect, but Walter is a pedophile. He has molested me all my life. I'm not the only one he's done this to. Aunt Cora, he has been doing these things to me since I was the age of 3. And, I know you know all about it. I am not the only one he has done this to. He has raped other girls as well, even our other sister, Sandra, in Liberia. The family needs to get him help."

"Now you gotta go. You've gone too far. Get outta my house!" shouted Aunt Cora.

Frustrated and knowing that Aunt Cora had turned a blind eye to Walter's problems, Brigitte told Aunt Cora, "Why you think my mom, your sister, is not around? He's the reason Mom never came back. Beatings which was to keep her quiet. She was scared of him. She got tired of it and never came back." And, turning towards her cousin, "How much is he paying you, Debra, to take the girls?" asked Brigitte.

"He's not paying me anything." answered Debra.

Looking around at everyone and then back at Brigitte, Walter told her, "I'm just taking the girls on a trip to their country."

Debra began to plead with her cousin, Brigitte. "I think it's time you regain a closer relationship with him. God said you should forgive, and he is trying to do the right thing. So should you."

Brigitte looked at her cousin with disgust. "Oh, here we go again with this God thing. Where was this God of yours when this monster was molesting me? Mom and her pastor confronted him, this man of God, and he denied every bit of it, and was too busy to discuss it. That so-called pastor did nothing, and for all I know, he was a pedophile, too. No one helped me."

Putting on an innocent face, Walter said, "I never did any of those things you are accusing me of. I never touched you or any other girl. What are you talking about?" Holding up both hands, he looked at Brigitte and then at everyone else in the kitchen.

"You fucking liar!!" shouted Brigitte. Aunt Cora grabbed her hand and led her straight to the door. Brigitte jerked her hand away and stormed out, slamming the screen door behind her.

Brigitte walked fast to her car, got in and screeched out of the driveway onto the streets. She pulled into her driveway in her Grey Chrysler, screeched on the brakes, threw the car in park, turned off the lights and hastily slammed the car door as she got out. She began to walk to and fro furiously. She rummaged through her desk and found a bottle of liquor. Sloppily pouring herself a glass, she downed the stiff drink. She put on Gothic music and turned on the surround-sound blasting the music, spinning and twirling around, screaming "Jonestown Tea" as she related to the lyrics. The pain was so deep that it was unbearable. The awful smell of his body against her innocent body, and the shame her father brought upon her. And then to top it off, her cousin agreed to let him take her daughters with him out of the country. It was unimaginable. Painful flashbacks of rapes and oral sex flooded her mind, and other abuse she suffered from her relatives. It was as if she was reliving that brutal life again and especially, while living in Monrovia, Liberia. She knew how hard it was to get out of Liberia. As a minor, she ran to the U. S. Embassy for help, but was returned to her father. He hid her passport and once she became an adult, refused to give it to her. She literally had to get the aid of the United States government to get her back into the United States. Going into her bathroom, she opened the cabinet and grabbed a bottle of pills. She poured several into her hand, downed them with her drink and within minutes, Brigitte passed out.

Back at a grimy-looking hotel, Walter thought about the events that had happened that day and paced back and forth. He wanted to talk to his daughter and was very nervous. After making several attempts to call her and no answer, he left a message. "Brigitte, please call me as soon as you get this message. We need to talk." Walter sat on the edge of his bed and rubbed his hands together. He knew he was faced with a major problem, and one that would not go away. He started to think back on his life and where he went wrong. He wondered what led to this behavior but, at the same time, not willing to admit that...

After Walter migrated to the United States as a young man, he became entangled with Shelia, Brigitte's mother, a fellow Liberian who was four years his junior. By the time she became pregnant with her first child, within one year, Walter was already cheating on her. He was a womanizer who liked lots of women especially small girls. He was even bold enough to bring some of them home. Once, when Shelia protested, he kicked her in the stomach and back. Despite the abuse and philandering, the couple had two more children together. One was Brigitte.

Both Shelia and Walter went in and out of relationships over many years. They each had many more children by multiple partners. Sheila had 16 children of whom 10 are still living. Walter had an unknown number of kids. Relatives estimate that he also had some in the teens. And neither had a history of taking particularly good care of their off-spring.

Leaving her children with a babysitter, Shelia went back to Liberia claiming to attend a funeral of a relative and stayed. Shelia stated she had no money to return, and the children were taken by Child Protective Services. Walter, who was known in the community as a successful businessman, went and picked up one child and later picked up three others. One was Brigitte. He took the children and left for Liberia, too. This was the turning point for Brigitte's life.

As the family slept upstairs, he would sneak three-year-old Brigitte downstairs into another room and rape her and have her perform oral sex on him. He would tell her that it was okay for him to do these things to her because he was her daddy, and these were things a daddy could do to get her ready for adulthood.

Still thinking, Walter knew the things Brigitte was talking about in Aunt Cora's house. He knew what he had done to those girls. But, how could he admit to such accusations and remain a free man, a free rich man. And, his family was on his side because he took care of everyone's welfare. No one wanted for anything.

CHAPTER 20

Everyone had their eyes on Brigitte as if in a hypnotic state. And, the judge and stenographer appeared to be frozen. Assante knew that he had the complete attention of everyone in the courtroom and asked Brigitte a question. "Brigitte, tell us, what got you so upset on the day of the family BBQ gathering? What made you so upset?"

"Flashbacks came to me as I was watching Walter bouncing my little cousin on his lap. He did the same thing to me. I know what he was doing," said Brigitte.

"What was he trying to do to her, Brigitte?" asked Assante.

Feeling ashamed, Brigitte said, "He was trying to stimulate her clitoris, so that she can feel all funny inside. If he sat you close to him on his lap, he wanted you to feel his hard penis. Then he would begin to whisper in your ear how much he loves you, and that fathers do this to show their love for their daughters."

Sounds of gasping could be heard throughout the courtroom. And the jurors were stunned at her testimony,

"How old were you when this first happened to you and for how long?" asked Assante.

"I was three years old when he started to rape and perform oral sex on me. He forced me to perform oral sex on him, too. And when I reached 16 years old, I was able to fight him off of me," said Brigitte.

"And where was your mother when all this was happening to you?" asked Assante.

"My mother abandoned me when I was two years old," Brigitte said. "But, when I was 12 years old, I went to live with my mother. I thought I would be happy and safe and I found out that living with her was unbearable. My mother took a rattan and beat me so hard that it left permanent marks on my body. I left and went back to live with my father. She told my father that I could not live with him because of the abuse. I denied it and convinced myself that it never happened," said Brigitte.

Assante then turned and walked over to the defense table where his assistant, Michael sat. Michael dressed in his brown suit and looking as sharp as Assante, knew that this was a very difficult case. He knew that the prosecutor was going to come full force to get a guilty verdict with plenty of time. And, as Assante was speaking, he handed him a video.

"Your Honor, I wish to have this video marked for identification as Defense Exhibit 1," said Assante.

Looking at Brigitte, he asked, "Do you recognize this video?"

"Yes," she said.

"You named this video 'My Reasons', correct?" asked Assante.

"What is on this video?" asked Assante.

"That's my confession for what I was about to do to him and my suicide. I planned to kill myself but wanted to explain why," said Brigitte.

"If I may, Your Honor, I'd like to play the video for the court," said Assante.

"You may proceed," said Judge Hamilton.

"If you are watching this video, then I'm probably dead. Before you judge me, my character, my life, walk down the path I have traveled. Sorrows, pain, fear, doubt, and hardly any laughter. Remember when something like this has happened, everyone has a story. And, I have a story. Please get all the facts before you judge; and when you have lived my life, then judge me."

Turning off the video, Assante walked over to Brigitte. "Ok, Brigitte, please finish your testimony."

"I was researching on my laptop," Brigitte explained.

"And please tell the court what you were researching," said Assante.

"I wasn't trying to kill him. I just wanted to stop him from using his penis to rip open little girl's wombs and forcing them to suck his dick till his filth came in their mouths. I was researching John Bobbitt and wanted to know what happened when his penis was cut off. I wanted to know how he survived and how it was reattached," said Brigitte. "But I saw a couple of other cases in China and Europe where the victim did not die. I looked at some scientific sites and learned how to successfully do it without killing him," she said.

"Did you do any other research?" sked Assante.

"Yes, I researched the statute of limitations of the crimes committed against me and the traumatic effects of sexual abuse on a child," said Brigitte. "I wanted help from the justice system. Yes, I wanted to go that route, but the statute of limitations said they couldn't do much about it. He had not touched me since I was 17, 18 in Africa which was not here. I couldn't go to them and say I think he's going to molest my cousins. I had no proof. My family's not backing me up. So, I'm thinking, stop him anyway you can. Somebody's got to do something. I knew he was not going to change," said Brigitte.

"Did you buy anything online?" asked Assante.

"Yes," stated Brigitte.

"And what did you buy?" asked Assante.

She answered, "Scalpels. A package of 50 on eBay for $6.83."

"What happened when he came to your apartment to talk to you?" asked Assante.

Brigitte took a deep breath and began to tell the story of that traumatic day.

CHAPTER 21

Brigitte finally returned her dad's phone call and learned that he wanted to discuss the issue that happened at Aunt Cora's house. Brigitte also wanted to confront her dad about the abuse he had inflicted on her as a child and the impact it now has on her as an adult. She wanted him to confess his abuse that he had inflicted on her. So that they may look each other in the face, she decided to invite him to come over. They agreed to meet at the train station.

On the day of their meeting, Brigitte decided to wear a nice blue blouse, jeans and tennis shoes. Walter wore an unbuttoned brown shirt exposing his chest with a gold chain, rings, brown slacks, a watch, and brown and crème-leather shoes. He acted as if he were trying to be sexy for Brigitte and trying to make an impression.

Now, while on the train, she noticed him looking at little girls no older than 10, but she held her tongue. Once they arrived at her apartment, she gave him a tour and offered him water. They both sat down and were facing each other.

"Well, do you know why we are here?" asked Brigitte.

"No why? You said you wanted to talk, so talk," said Walter.

Very nervous, she began from the beginning telling him about the first time he forced himself on top of her and the phone ringing. "You were trying to rape me. I was crying and telling you to stop."

Walter looked at her in disbelief and said, "How do you even remember that? Weren't you three years old?"

Brigitte thought to herself, *This is his response. Wow! Not shock, not denial just casual dismissal.* Beginning to get pissed, she spoke about the times from when she was four to 17, the oral sex and the effect the abuse had on her as a child being in constant pain, shame, and fear. It led to early masturbation. He continued to deny the abuse. Brigitte also mentioned the porn he forced her to watch.

Walter dissembled and began to use some of the same excuses he had used in the past. "I was only teaching you to clean yourself."

Brigitte then asked him, "Do you remember New Year's Eve, 1997? Sandra was asleep and you attempted a sexual attack on her. I was asleep and woke up in the middle of the night only to find that you were performing oral sex on me. At first, I experienced some sort of pleasure. I didn't know what was going on, and then I realized it was you. And, for the first time I fought you off of me. I was crying and you gave up."

Walter suddenly interrupted her. "Well, the reason why I wanted to talk to you is because of something that happened in Africa with Sandra, your half-sister, who is back in Liberia, and now about 18 years old, had been gang-raped as a child during the years you lived there with her. It's your fault that no one had been told about it earlier."

Brigitte's first thought was that this was a lie. One that would play on her guilt and serve as an alibi if Sandra ever claimed to be abused by him and also get some of the attention off of him. But, all that did was make Brigitte a victim all over again. It tapped into all the emotions that she had been harboring for weeks. Self-loathing, guilt, and rage. She had told Sandra that she would be back for her and get her out of there. Now, a decade later, the fact that she wasn't able to keep her promise stills weighed on her.

Brigitte looked at her father with disgust and told him, "I invited you to come here, so that I could ask you not to take my cousins to Liberia. You and I both know what you intend to do, and it is wrong. When I walked into that house and saw my cousin sitting on your knee, I had flashbacks. You bouncing her like you were really enjoying every bit of the bounce. This shit needs to stop. So, why not start today by admitting what you did to me and how wrong it was. Since you want to make amends, admit what you did, and that it was wrong." Walter looked around and then at Brigitte.

"What! What is it you feel I have done to you? All these years. You liked it. I could tell. I have not done anything wrong, and besides, you liked it and you know it," said Walter.

"I didn't like SHIT! Did you ever stop to think that a grown-ass man's dick your size going inside me, a little girl at the age of three, would rip me open, cause extreme excruciating pain and not to mention may not ever have a normal life or children? Huh, oh nooo, you haven't. Well, let me show you what it felt like Mr. Man!" shouted Brigitte.

The air in the room was becoming very thick and the mood had changed. Brigitte flew into a rage. She began yelling and calling him a liar. She now was at the point of no return. She realized he had no intentions of changing, and the girls were in danger. He needed to be stopped as she angrily glared him up and down. "You knew what you did was wrong!" she told him.

Walter stood up and took a step toward her. She reached for the pepper spray she kept clipped to her belt. She shouted, "I hope this shit does enough damage so that you can't even look at a young girl ever again!"

They fought and fell to the floor. The coffee table broke. She overpowered him knowing that her security guard training had come to some use. He fell to the floor landing on his back. She looked for a way to restrain him and found the handcuffs she had bought after her friends teased her about her job as a rent-a-cop. As Brigitte put the handcuffs on Walter, he began to scream. Now in full panic, she quickly ran to the bathroom and grabbed a towel. She stuffed it in his mouth, wrapped his mouth with duct tape and pulled down his pants. Brigitte got up and went towards her desk. She reached into the drawer and grabbed some scissors. She tried those first because that was the first thing she saw on the web site but, they did not work. She then retrieved the box of scalpels from inside the desk. Walter was lying still at that point. One cut was enough. There was not a lot of blood.

Looking down at him, Brigitte asked, "Tell me. How are you feeling now? Does this feel good too, Daddy? Is Daddy hard yet, huh?"

Brigitte thought he was still alive and continued to talk to Walter even though he lay still. "Oh, you can't talk. My bad. Just like I couldn't talk every time you stuck your funky dick in my mouth."

"Pedophiles like you will cause little girls like Kayla and Dena lots of psychological trauma, guilt, and depression. Pedophiles like you cause so many problems. I bet you didn't know about psychological problems, trauma, guilt, and depression. I was ashamed of myself for the things you made me do. Did you know that? Huh? You victimized me for years, you stupid rotten, dirty, mother fucker. This shit is going to stop, and you are not doing that shit to my little cousins. This fuckin' abuse stops today!" shouted Brigitte.

COURT ROOM

The judge, jurors and audience in the courtroom have their eyes on her as if in a trance and mouths were frozen open. The courtroom was quiet.

Looking at the jurors, Assante asked, "Was he alive when you called 911?"

Brigitte felt remorse for what she had done, but knew she must answer his questions. Wringing her hands, she answered "Yes, he was," she said with tears falling down her face.

Assante asked looking at Brigitte, "So, he was alive when you called 911?"

"Yes," she said as she wiped the tears from her face.

"No further questions, Your Honor," said Assante.

The judge looked towards Hayes. "Do you wish to cross-examine, Hayes?"

"Yes Your Honor," said Hayes.

She got up and walked towards Brigitte, looking at her with a stern face.

"You stated, and let me paraphrase, that you were so upset that you immediately left the family gathering and went home. Is this correct?" asked Hayes.

"Yes," Brigitte said.

"And, due to psychological effects and the harm he caused you, you had to stop him," stated Hayes.

Brigitte said, "Yes."

"You went home and researched on your computer the results of castration on a man because you had to stop him. Am I correct?" asked Hayes.

"Yes," said Brigitte.

"Well, did you not know that if a man is castrated, hand-cuffed, towel in his mouth, and duct tape around his mouth and neck and pepper spray in his eyes that he would die?" asked Hayes.

"No, that was not my intention," said Brigitte as she looked towards Assante.

Attorney Hayes then asked about the scalpels. "You say you ordered the scalpels on Ebay? Correct?"

"Yes," replied Brigitte.

Looking at the jury Attorney Hayes asked, "But why so many? Fifty, I think, was correct."

"Yes, I just bought them by the box. No particular reason," replied Brigitte.

Looking towards the judge, Hayes said, "No further questions, Your Honor." She turned around and went back to her seat. The judge looked at Brigitte. "You may step down and go back to your seat."

Judge Hamilton looked at both attorneys. "Are there any other witnesses you wish to examine?"

They each said, "No, Your Honor."

"You may begin your closing arguments," stated Judge Hamilton.

Prosecuting attorney, Julia Hayes, got up and faced the jurors. "Ladies and gentlemen of the jury, I must reiterate again, 'a very serious crime has been committed.' Brigitte knew exactly what she was doing. She became angry at a family gathering due to Walter bouncing her cousin on his knee. She accused him of his sexual acts committed on her and her cousin. She leaves the gathering and goes home to do research. Research with the intent to do bodily harm to Walter. She invites him over and tells him he needs to stop his wrongdoings on her and other little girls. Brigitte was consumed with vengeance towards her father. Her video even states that she is giving a reason for what she has done. She planned and ordered scalpels off the Internet to use in her act of vengeance. Ladies and gentlemen of the jury, all the evidence points to a guilty conviction of first degree murder." Hayes turned and walked back to her seat.

Assante got up and walked towards the jury.

"Ladies and gentlemen of the Jury, Brigitte Harris is not guilty of murder. She suffered throughout her childhood severe physical, mental, and sexual abuse. She is guilty of defending herself and other helpless and defenseless young girls. Review the facts that Brigitte lived with every moment of her life."

He walked over to an easel board and with the assistance of Attorney Michaels, he placed pictures of little babies and children on the board. He then asked the jurors to close their eyes.

"I ask you to place yourself in her position experiencing something that a child should not ever experience. She was forced to experience feelings that only adults should experience. As adults, we know what sex is and the accompanying feelings associated with it. Imagine a baby or child who is forced into sex and oral sex. Their little bodies not even mature enough to take the force of an adult, and, not even mature enough to accept or reject good or bad feelings."

Assante tells them to now open their eyes and pointed to pictures of a baby and states, "Let's just say at three years old, she knew what it was like to give birth. And if she became pregnant at nine years old, can you even imagine giving birth to a child? Can you even imagine the pain? As Dr. Warner's testimony showed, this girl suffered from mixed and confused feelings forced upon her. Brigitte Harris suffered post-traumatic stress syndrome, depression, and somatization disorder. And with this disorder, she built up a defense against the psychological pain.

How well do we know the people who are close to us—family, friends, teachers, and, yes, the clergy? Walter was someone's father, son, uncle, husband, grandfather, brother and coworker. I'm sure these people had no idea he was a pedophile. Shocking isn't it? Most people think you look the part or this type of behavior only happens in certain cultures. It happens everywhere. Walter should have been a father to her and nurturing fatherly love, not using his daughter for his sexual whims. She does not deny what has happened. She is not a cold-blooded killer. She was defending herself. She knew in her heart if she committed suicide without doing something, this abuse would continue. No one could stop him. Not her mother or a pastor. And to make matters worse, if he was convicted of the crimes, he would have fallen under the Intrafamilial Law. Do you know what that is? Better yet, it is known as 'incest exception,' incest exception literally rewards perpetrators for birthing their own victims. Since he bore his victim, the charges would be less than if he were a stranger. This is absurd. In many states, and also in New York, family members plead down from a Class B felony (sexually violating a child, with a sentence of twenty-plus years in prison) to 'incest,' a Class E felony with the possibility of probation, if convicted."

Assante looked at the jury, paused, and then continued, "As ridiculous as this law may sound, it has to stop. I plead with you that when you deliberate on this case, keep in mind the awful life she had to endure all alone as a child. This crime does not warrant a life conviction. Even U. S. Senator Chuck Schumer, New York State Senators Diane J. Savino and Eric Adams and the mayor wrote letters on her behalf asking that she not be convicted of this crime. Please show this lady leniency today and come back with a verdict of innocent."

He then turned and walked back to his table with Brigitte and Attorney Michaels.

After both attorneys gave their final arguments to the jury, Judge Hamilton looked gravely at the jury and began to speak, "You have the instructions. Do not discuss with any non-juror anything relating to the evidence in the trial or to the deliberations of the jury. I admonish you once again to not make your rulings based on emotions, but rather on the evidence and facts presented today. You have two manslaughter charges to review and decide. First and second degree manslaughter and second-degree murder."

The jury further understood that a conviction of second-degree murder may be downgraded to first-degree manslaughter on the grounds of "extreme emotional disturbance." That is, that the perpetrator had been somehow driven to act by what he or she perceived as a legitimate threat, or if she or he had been provoked into an act of self-defense.

"You are dismissed." Then, BANG! He hits the gavel. The jury was sequestered and headed to the jury deliberating room.

CHAPTER 22

NEXT DAY – COURT ROOM

In a packed standing-room-only courtroom, the jury entered showing no expressions with poker faces. Brigitte sat on the defense side of the court room, wearing a white sweater and skirt. With tears in her eyes, she looked at her relatives sitting behind her trying to memorize each of their faces. At that moment, the judge walked into the courtroom.

"All rise. Queens Court for the 11th Judicial District is in session. The Honorable Judge Hamilton presiding."

Judge Hamilton entered the courtroom.

"Good morning, everyone. You may be seated. Has the jury agreed on a verdict?"

"We have, Your Honor," and the foreman juror, handed the verdict to the bailiff. The bailiff walked over to Judge Hamilton and handed him the verdict. The judge read the verdict, handed it back to the bailiff, who handed it back to the foreman juror to read the verdict.

Judge Hamilton looked towards the defense. "Brigitte Harris, will you please rise for the reading of the verdict?"

Looking back towards the foreman juror, the judge asked, "What is the verdict with the case: State of New York vs. Brigitte Harris for the charge of murdering Walter Harris as charged by the prosecution?"

The foreman juror read out loud, "We the jurors find the accused, Brigitte Harris, not guilty of second-degree murder; not guilty of first-degree manslaughter; Guilty of second-degree manslaughter."

The courtroom was in an uproar. Spectators were expressing joys of happiness and some of anger.

Each of Brigitte's attorneys grabbed and hugged her. Brigitte let out a sigh of relief and smiled. Her brother Tyson, Sheena, and Aunt Glo were confused and didn't realize what had just happened. They thought she was going to be found not guilty on all counts. She will not get the life sentence or death sentence. The prosecuting attorney expressed discontent, and the judge pounded the gavel. "Order in the court, order in the court." Everyone in the courtroom became quiet. Judge Hamilton continued, "Sentencing will be as follows: Brigitte Harris you will be confined to the Bedford Hills Correctional Facility for a term of 5 to 15 years with a possibility of parole. Court is adjourned!" and he hit the gavel, BANG!

Judge Hamilton got up from the bench and left the courtroom; and then the jurors left. Two rugged female jail guards walked over to Brigitte and handcuffed her. Brigitte, showing no emotion, was taken away.

"Brigitte, don't worry we will appeal," declared Assante.

"Okay, please do what you can. Thank you," said Brigitte.

Assante and Michaels gathered up all their documents and belongings and prepared to leave the courtroom. Hayes glared at Assante and said, "Guess there's no real winners here."

As he glared back at Hayes, Assante said, "Yes, there is a winner. Second degree manslaughter as opposed to murder in the first."

"She will do all fifteen and guaranteed," Hayes said with a smirk on her face.

Assante told her, "We will see about that. Excuse me," as he and Michaels both brushed past her and left the courtroom.

CHAPTER 23

LOS ANGELES – 4 YEARS LATER

Sipping on soda and eating popcorn, Terri sat mesmerized as she watched one of her favorite crime documentary shows. The commentator caught her attention as she talked about the infamous case in Rockaway, Queens County, New York concerning Brigitte Harris, a girl who was sexually molested by her father. Brigitte cried out, "but no one cared." She got no love and needed help. And, as Terri listened and took notes, she decided to write a letter to Brigitte to see if she would respond. She expressed her own traumatic experience and wanted to become Brigitte's pen pal with the hope that they could heal each other.

Two weeks later and looking for her unemployment check in the mail, Terri listened attentively for footsteps from the mail carrier and the flapping noise of her mailbox. Unemployment had made her very nervous, but to keep herself busy, she sat down in her brown antique chair and began to type vigorously on her computer. She knew her unemployment benefits would soon run out. She must find employment.

Suddenly, Terri heard the mail carrier. She jumped up and ran to get her mail. Disappointment instantly hit her when the unemployment check was not there, but then a smile came over her face as a letter from Brigitte Harris was in the box. Terri sat on the floor, opened the letter and began to read it. Brigitte thanked Terri for writing to her and expressed that she didn't get much mail from strangers. She told Terri she would love to be her pen pal. After reading the letter, Terri ran upstairs and called her producer friend, Leonard Powers. Terri explained to him that she had reached out to Brigitte Harris and briefly told him about her story and of the abuse she also suffered. Leonard Powers never knew this about Terri. She explained to him that she had an idea for a movie and wanted to meet with him. He agreed.

Terri relaxed with a lemonade sitting on the couch in the meeting room. She knew she had to convince Leonard that this would make a great movie. She told him, "Leonard, a few weeks ago I was watching this crime documentary show and they were talking about the life of Brigitte Harris. I wrote to her and guess what? She wrote back to me. I have become pen pals with her. But now I have an idea. I know that I'm working on our script, but I want to do a movie about her."

As Leonard sat down next to her, he wondered if Brigitte's life story was important enough to make a movie. "Well, what's her story about?" asked Leonard.

"Childhood abuse, the accidental killing of her father, and a wrongful sentence that does not justify the conviction. I feel that I can do this. We want to send a message and make the public aware of this dark subject. And this would also give me the chance to become a director that creates movies with meaning," Terri said.

Agreeing with her, Leonard said, "Sounds like a good story-line, but the first thing you need to do is get her permission, and get her to give you the exclusive rights."

Excited about her idea, she also said, "I'll ask her and explain the purpose. I'll let you know as soon as she replies. Many children can be helped with this movie. Imagine the number of children who are suffering right now and can be saved as we speak."

CHAPTER 24

Today was mail day, and Brigitte looked forward to receiving mail. When she got her mail, she noticed a letter from her new pen pal, Terri. She sat down on the bed, opened the letter and smiled.

"*Hello, Brigitte, hope all is well with you today. I want to tell you a little more about myself and my profession. I have been in the film industry for fourteen years, and I am a script supervisor. With my talent, I would love to tell our stories through a movie. It's not about the crime you committed. I have been doing major research on the subject of sexual abuse towards children and know that the public needs to be made aware of the seriousness of this problem in the world today.*

The world needs our help. The facts state that 90 percent of children molested know their molesters, as stated in the National Child Abuse Statistics. In the "Voicing Abuse Project," one in three girls and one in six boys are sexually abused before the age of 18. And to make matters worse, only 1 to 10 percent are ever disclosed, making

78

child molestation one of the most underreported crimes. I know we can make a difference, and this is our opportunity to be bold and daring, to expose with no fear this gravely dark evil, so that other children will not be afraid to come forth for help. Please let me know your thoughts."

CHAPTER 25

LOS ANGELES

Terri sat on her patio enjoying her oceanic view and checking her bank account when suddenly she heard a knock on her door. She saw that it was her apartment manager, Titus Grant, and cringed for she knew that her rent was past due. Terri opened the door and let him inside her apartment.

"Terri, hi how are you?" asked Titus.

"Not too good right now. I know that my rent is due, but I'm low on funds. And I don't want to be evicted."

"Well, I'll do my best to slow up the process, but you need to hurry and get the money. The attorneys are filing an eviction in the courts, just to give you heads up," said Titus.

"I'm working on it. Thanks," said Terri.

After he left, and knowing that her funds were exhausted, she broke down and cried.

A few weeks later, a U-Haul truck was parked in front of Terri's apartment, and two big Hispanic men were loading her furniture and belongings onto the truck. Terri was crying, not wanting to leave her beautiful beachfront apartment. She took one final walk through the apartment and then walked out the door. Realizing that she was about to venture into a zone that may have her struggling for a while, but knowing she couldn't afford to pay anyone to put this project together, she decided to teach herself everything she needed to know about productions, budgets, and directing. She was willing to make the sacrifice.

She saw Titus waiting for her at the truck and, with tears in her eyes, she walked up to him and gave him a hug. "Thank you so much for everything you have done for me. Titus, you are a wonderful man, and I will never forget you," Terri said

"I have never met anyone like you. And with the determination you have, you will be successful. Just keep doing what you are doing," said Titus.

"I will, and I will stay in touch," said Terri.

He gave her a hug and wished her well. Terri turned around and jumped into the truck. Not looking back, she drove down the street out of his sight and pulled over to the side. Her cries were uncontrollable. Terri was homeless and refused to call her relatives due to pride. Picking up her cell phone, she called her friend, Beverly.

CHAPTER 26

Dressed in an orange jumpsuit, Brigitte sat across from Assante. He pulled out a book of forms, pertaining to her parole hearing.

Assante folded his hands on the table. "Sorry it's taken so long for me to get back to see you. As you know I have been preparing for your parole hearing. How's it going for you in here?"

Brigitte sat across from him watching him place documents on the table. "I'm good. No problems. Just doing what I'm told."

"Well, the law does say that the Parole Commission may grant parole if an inmate has substantially observed the rules of the institution, but here are a few things that will need to be included," Assante said.

As he is slid an application in front of her, he explained what they needed to do to proceed with the parole. "You must fill this out. Then sign for parole. Everyone who wishes to be considered for parole must complete this application."

Assante looked at Brigitte as she reviewed the form. "As you can see I have filled in most of the pertinent information. You can fill in what I have missed."

Brigitte looked at Assante. "What actually happens at a parole hearing?"

Assante explained, "The hearing is an opportunity for you to tell your own story and to express your own thoughts as to why you feel you should be paroled. Many things may come up, such as the details of your offense and your prior criminal history. Also your accomplishments in the institution may also be brought up, as well as any problems you have had to meet in the past or are likely to face in the future.

The Parole Commission is interested both in the protection of society against further criminal behavior as well as your needs as an individual. You also have rights," said Assante.

Brigitte asked, "Do I need a release plan?"

Assante told her, "Yes. Your release plan should definitely include a suitable residence and a verified offer of employment."

"I will work on that. Ahrite, I know our time is done. I will call you with that information as soon as I get it. I just can't thank you enough," Brigitte said.

"Oh, by the way," Brigitte burst out, "I have a pen pal who wants to help me and do a movie about sexual abuse that can possibly help others. What do you think about that?"

"Well, you know we turned down the Discovery Channel's offer to tell your story. Are you sure you want to do this now?" he asked.

Brigitte replied, "Yes, I do."

Assante then said, "Okay, it's all up to you. It's your decision. I will back you if need be. Have her contact me."

As the guard came in to escort her back to the cell, Brigitte stood up with a happy look on her face and said, "Okay, I will write her back and let her know." Assante watched them both as they walked through the doors.

As Brigitte walked down the corridor, she thought about what Assante had discussed with her, *I can't believe my parole hearing has finally come up. I need to write Terry a letter and let her know that I have a parole hearing coming up and we can do the movie. I will ask her to help me find a place to live and a job. I may be able to live with a relative, but a job is another thing. Who would hire me?*

CHAPTER 27

LOS ANGELES

Terri's friend, Beverly Connors, was a full-figured woman with a pretty face, light-skinned with long, wavy hair. She had known her for years and was very thankful that she allowed her to come stay at her home. Beverly's charming home was located in the Richland Farm area in Compton, California, where horses grazed on the land and beautiful garden landscapes covered yards.

Looking out the window, Terri thought about what the future may hold for her with producing and directing a movie for the first time in her life. Her friend, Beverly, allowed her to stay so that she could get back on her feet. She set aside a place in the corner of her den for Terri to work on her script about Brigitte's story.

Working non-stop on her script, Terri decided to take a break. Stretching her arms and rubbing her neck, she looked back at her computer and went to *Facebook* to see if there were any updates from groups for Brigitte Harris. There was a group, but it had been three years since any updates were posted. She knew Brigitte's parole was coming up, so she reactivated one of the groups as administrator and named the group "Free Brigitte Harris." She wanted to get as many supporters as possible.

The next day, she looked at the page and saw that New York City Public Advocate Sallie Elkordy, wanted to talk to her and left her number for her to call back. She immediately picked up the phone and called Ms.Elkordy.

"Hello, is this Sallie?"

"Yes, is this Terri?" asked Sallie.

"Yes, this is Terri. How are you? And thank you for reaching out to me," said Terri.

"Terri, I was wondering what happened with this website? When it first went up, I posted a letter from Governor David Paterson in reference to his support for Brigitte. Can I have your e-mail address? I'll send you the letter," stated Sallie.

"Yes, and I will get as many supporters as I can to write the parole board in favor of releasing Brigitte," said Terri.

"Terri, I have been following her story from day one. And I was initially shocked when that under-paid judge gave her five to fifteen years. Let me know what I can do, and I will do whatever I can to support you," said Sallie.

Terri hung up the phone thinking, *"Oh my God! I am so happy to know that New York City Public Advocate, Sallie Elkordy is one of Brigitte's supporters. I've got to work on those websites and write Brigitte a letter, too. I need to let her know that she has supporters out here who are ready to help her."*

LOS ANGELES – NEXT MORNING

After being at Beverly's for six months, Terri was sitting at the table eating bacon and waffles for breakfast when her friend, Beverly, walked in with a man behind her. He was nicely built, a caramel-colored brother, tatted up and wearing a wife beater, a tank top T-shirt.

"Morning, Terri," said Beverly.

As Terri responded, "Good morning," she wondered, *"Who is this man?"*

She noticed that he had placed a duffel bag on the floor that appeared to be full of clothes.

JOHNSON, SHANNON, PATTERSON

"Terri, this is my man, Tony Billings," and then suddenly Beverly became quiet, grabbed her man's hand and looked away. Looking at her friend and wondering what was going on, Tony looked directly at Terri and began to speak.

"I know my girl is yo dawg, but I'm back to stay, and she won't be able to give you a place to stay anymore, 'cause she won't be paying the bills. I will, and I can't afford you. Don't mean to be so blunt. But you understand the game, don't you?" asked Tony.

"Yes! I got it! Get out. That part right there," said Terri.

And looking at Beverly, "I'll leave right now. I will be back this weekend to get my things!"

Terri got up from the table, slammed her fork down, and caused the waffles and bacon to fall on the floor. Looking at Beverly, Terri shook her head and walked out of the room.

LOS ANGELES – THAT DAY

Terri headed towards downtown Los Angeles wearing a red T-shirt, sandals, and a jacket. She had her purse, one bag of clothes and toiletries. She barely scraped up enough money to ride the bus and metro train from Compton to downtown Los Angeles. *I should have asked them for some money since they wanted me out.* She had to get to the Los Angeles Homeless Mission as soon as possible and before it got too late.

The closer she got to the Mission, the worse the downtown area neighborhood looked. Homelessness was seen on both sides of the street. People living in cardboard homes, makeshift homes all along the sidewalks, as if people had claimed their own territories. So many people were headed towards the Mission. Reality kicking in, feeling alone and hurt, Terri headed toward the end of the line, waiting for her turn to talk to someone regarding shelter. *What is happening to me? What am I going to do? People whom I thought were my friends really are not. I don't have a dime in my pocket, but I have a cause and a test. Can I handle this?* Then she thought, *I must handle this. Brigitte is depending on me. I don't want to be the one who lets her down.* She remembered Leonard telling her the journey would be hard, and asked her if she would be able to handle it. With tears in her eyes, she stood patiently, waiting to talk to someone. Finally, her turn came. The Mission referred her to the Nu-Image Shelter. She had to ride the bus to get to that location and before a set time. Using a bus transfer, she hurried to get in line so as not to miss the bus, or she would be sleeping in one of those cardboard boxes. She hopped on the bus again and headed towards the shelter with all the derelicts—smelly people who hadn't bathed in days and wanted to get to the shelter just for baths and food.

LOS ANGELES – THAT EVENING

Sitting inside Nu Image waiting her turn to be called for intake processing at the shelter, Terri finally heard her name over the intercom. "Terri Johnson, room 3." There in room 3 was Chauncey Eubanks, a well-dressed black, white shirt, black pants, multicolored tie, very handsome man who eyed her up and down.

Now why is she here? Chauncey thought. *She's clean and her eyes are swollen from crying.*

"Are you Terri Johnson?" asked Chauncey.

"Yes," said Terri.

"My name is Chauncey Eubanks." He shook her hand. "So, Ms. Johnson, this must be your first time here because I don't recognize your face. And, you look like you don't belong here. You look lost."

"Yes. This is my first time here, and I only want to rent a room somewhere. I was told to come her first and then you could help me get placed in low-income housing," said Terri.

"Well, if you need transitional housing you will have to go through this intake one time....."

"Don't mean to cut you off. Can you recommend someone?" asked Terri.

"The normal process is for you to stay here overnight. Then, you can be placed. I will make an exception for you. I will sign you in, and you can leave now if you don't want to stay. I will place you with Marilyn Carter, a housing manager," said Chauncey.

"That's great, but I have no money. Not even for the bus. Is transitional housing shared living?" asked Terri.

"Yes, it is, but it's better than this. As far as the money, we used to give bus tokens, but not anymore. I'll give you some bus fare." Reaching into his pocket, he handed her two dollars in change and Marilyn Carter's business card.

"Thank you so much, but I will stay. I'm tired and hungry. I just want to get off my feet. They are killing me. I will leave in the morning," said Terri.

"Okay." And with a look of warning, he tells her, "Keep all your belongings with you and sleep on top of your purse. Trust no one."

"Wow, like that? Lord, please give me strength," said Terri.

As Terri walked over to the women's side of the shelter, she felt light-headed and dizzy. Vertigo had kicked in, and she was very, very tired. All Terri wanted to do was just eat, lie down and get some much-needed rest and sleep. She received her lunch consisting of bread, chicken, mashed potatoes, salad and juice. Nearly dropping her tray, she managed to find a table where she sat down and ate. Looking around she saw women like herself that didn't look like they belonged there. This made her feel a little better realizing other women like her were enduring the night.

After eating, she found an empty cot, sat down, and surveyed her surroundings. Her feet were dirty, but she knew there was no need to take a shower as the women there were nasty looking. She realized that there were drug addicts, thieves, abused women, prostitutes, and homeless people. She lay down with her bag of belongings underneath her knees and her purse under her pillow. She took a deep breath, closed her eyes and fell asleep.

CHAPTER 28

Working in the kitchen, Brigitte served food to her fellow inmates. One inmate tried to test Brigitte and talked about the way food was served on her tray and the threat of cutting someone up. Sandra looked at Brigitte. "Bitch, you need to watch how you putting food on my tray."

Brigitte glared at the girl. "Don't fuck with me, 'cause I ain't in the mood. In fact, move yo ass on."

"What you gonna do, Bitch? Cut my fucking balls off?" Sandra said.

Brigitte gave her an 'I'll beat your ass look,' rolled her eyes and continued to serve the next person. Other inmates laughed. She knew that if she reacted she may mess up her parole. Brigitte was too close to freedom to let some punk girl destroy that for her.

Another inmate, Ronnie, baited Brigitte, too. "Do we have any bar-b-que grills up in here?" Ronnie said.

"Naw, no grills, and no weenies," responded Marcy, another inmate.

Brigitte gave them a big cheesy smile with a fuck-you look.

"Ladies, keep it moving," said a gray-haired female guard.

CHAPTER 29

The next morning, Terri caught the bus and met Marilyn Carter at the transitional house she was placed at. She was greeted at the door by a stocky, serious-looking black woman in a casual business dress. Her hair weave was long and flowing. She wore heavy makeup and lots of loud gaudy jewelry. "Hello, come on in. Are you Terri Johnson?"

"Yes."

"I am Marilyn Carter, the owner and house manager of 'Shelter for You.' "

Following Marilyn into her office, Terri saw that the house was nicely decorated in black, white, and red contemporary furniture.

"Chauncey told me all about you, and that I should give you a chance. You don't look like a drug addict, an abused woman, or a hooker, so what's your story?"

Terri closed her eyes and slightly shook her head. She opened her eyes and looked at Marilyn and began her story.

"In pursuit of my dreams, I was laid off from work, evicted from my ocean-view apartment, unemployment ran out, no car, lost my storage containing all my belongings and given the boot from someone whom I thought was my friend. I've hit the bottom of the barrel. At the same time, I am choosing to help someone to regain her life, stability and freedom; I'm losing mine in the process. The only thing I still have left in my life are my kids and grandchildren. And I am scared to tell them what has happened. All their childhood memories were lost in my storage unit. And I don't think they will ever forgive me. I am a script writer, and Brigitte Harris, the person whom I am trying to help, has given me the exclusive rights to tell her story through a movie. And because of the abuse that we both experienced as children, I want to start a nonprofit organization for sexually-abused children. I'm also assisting her with her upcoming parole. She has a chance to be free. I've got to help her, and all I need is a little help, work, and a place to sleep."

"Does your family know?" asked Marilyn.

"No, and I have family and friends, but I'm tired of asking them for help. They can't see or understand my dream and want me to get a job. So, I've chosen what I am doing now. I was shot and almost died. Through God's grace, he spared my life and for a reason—to make a difference for myself, Brigitte, and all the little children of the world," said Terri.

Marilyn watched Terri attentively, but was very impressed with her story.

Terri continued, "I am currently on general relief, receiving $200 a month and $200 in food stamps. That's all I have right now. But, if you give me a place to stay, I can work off the difference if you have work. I need someone right now to help me, and believe in me."

"Well, you know, believe it or not, I was in your shoes once. While in pursuit of my dreams, I was in a shelter for a day. I slept on a bus stop bench for months outside with a baby. A lady I didn't even know came up to us and said I could live with her to get this baby off the street. And so I did. A stranger helped me. So I'm going to help you," said Marilyn.

Marilyn paused while watching Terri. "I like you. There's something about you that says I should give you a chance. I will help you. I will only charge you $500 for rent. You keep your food stamps. You also need a cell phone. And I will get you one.

I do have some office work I could use some help with. So, you can work off $300 of your rent, and I will make sure you have some pocket change."

"Thank you so much. I'm almost finished with the script, but I also need a 501©(3)for my nonprofit organization. To be tax-exempt under section 501©(3) of the Internal Revenue Code, my organization must be and operated exclusively for exempt purposes and none of its earnings may inure to any private shareholder or individual. Can you help me with that?" asked Terri.

"Yes, I can help you with that. Come follow me, and I will show you your room. You will share your room with Jennifer, and here's the key. The other ladies who live here will be here in a little while. Here's the bathroom, laundry room, and garage. Go on and get yourself settled in. Come to my office in the morning, and we will get started," said Marilyn.

"Thank you so much, and may God bless you. I haven't had a shower in two days, and now I am going to take a long, hot shower," said Terri.

For the first time in weeks, Terri felt like her world was not ending, and that maybe she could help Brigitte and herself after all. She almost skipped to the bathroom, praising God for his mercy and making a mental to-do list.

LOS ANGELES – NEXT DAY

Reaching the office of Marilyn in "Shelter for You," and looking rested, happy, and excited, Terri said, "Good morning, Marilyn. Sorry I'm late," as she entered the door. "I was connecting with some supporters for Brigitte."

Going through the mail and documents on her desk, Marilyn asked, "Anything that's going to benefit her release?"

"Yes, approximately three-hundred-and-fifty Africans wrote letters to their Embassy on behalf of Brigitte. I hope they get here in time for the parole. Sallie spoke with New York State Assemblyman William Scarborough, and he also is writing his letter in support of Brigitte. I'm going to call the senators, governor, mayor and her parole officer and ask for their support of Brigitte," said Terri as she watched Marilyn separate her mail.

Marilyn asked, "You're calling them? Why not ask Sallie since she has inside connections?"

"They are no different than me. I may be nobody to them, but I'm somebody to someone. I'm determined to take them on for what I believe in, and my cause," responded Terri.

"Now, that's what I'm talking about. A woman with an attitude. I like that," stated Marilyn.

"The same month I got shot was the same month Brigitte committed her crime. I'm here for a reason, and God spared me for this purpose. The parole board need to know that Brigitte will have a place to stay and a job when she is released. I spoke to Mother Mary at "Steps to End Family Violence," and she said that they will take care of everything. She is going to fax the confirmation to me regarding the shelter and a job for Brigitte. Is it okay that it comes here?" Terri said.

"Sure, it's okay. It's the same number you called the office on. She must call you first before she sends a fax," said Marilyn.

"Ok, thanks," said Terri.

"Since your hands are full right now, I will start on your articles for your non-profit organization. It's gonna take a little time. So, I got you, don't worry," said Marilyn.

"Thank you. So, what do you need me to help you with?" asked Terri.

"You can start with that tray over there. Those are bills that need to be filed. And answer the phones like this: 'Shelter for You. How may I direct your call?' Take messages and make appointments. My itinerary is very important, so stay on top of it," said Marilyn.

Marilyn showed Terri around the office and gave her a few more tasks to accomplish. Terri knew she could do this job, and while she was busy filing papers and answering phones, she could not stop planning her future.

NEW YORK

Walking outside after a day's work from his job, Tyson Harris, Brigitte's brother, dark-skinned with dreads, and dressed in a nice outfit whistled while making his way to his black Range Rover truck. *I wonder what's going on with my sister. I sure do miss her.* He pulled out his cell phone and started scrolling down the apps. Briefly skimming from one social network to another, he decided to pull up the defunct group, "Free Brigitte Harris." His eyes grew big and his heart skipped a beat. The group had been reactivated and with a new administrator, Terri Johnson. And, to his surprise, Brigitte had many followers in support of her. He immediately sent a friend request to Terri.

LOS ANGELES

Terri and her roommate, Jennifer Perkins, a younger dark-skinned lady with rollers in her hair were sleeping in each of their full-size beds. A ringing noise blasted loudly in the air.

Ring! Ring! Ring! And in her own deep sleep, Terri realized that the computer component magic jack was ringing. That was the only way Terri could receive collect calls from Brigitte from jail. So, Terri knew who it was. Jumping out of bed and throwing the covers off, she rushed over to the phone. "Hello"

There was an operator on the other line. "You have a collect call from Brigitte Harris. Do you accept the charges?"

"Yes, I do," said Terri.

The call was connected. "Hello, Terri?"

"Yes, Brigitte. How are you?" asked Terri.

"I'm good and . . ." But as Brigitte continued with the conversation, she let Terri know her parole was granted. Terri suddenly shouted, "Yes, yes. Thank God. Yes. I'm sorry for screaming in your ear. Girl, I'm just happy for you. Oh my God, time to celebrate," said Terri.

As Brigitte's phone time came to a close, Terri answered her. "Ok, honey, call me in a couple of days, so we can plan for your release. Writing that down right now, August 13, 2012. I'm gonna notify all of our supporters. Big congrats, talk to you soon," said Terri.

Hanging up the phone, Terri turned around and saw that Jennifer woke up and heard the whole conversation. Sitting up in her bed, Jennifer clapped her hands and waved them in the air, as she rejoiced with her. "Oh my God, Terri, great job."

Terri turned on her computer and went straight to the Free Brigitte Harris group. More good news. She saw Tyson's friend request. She accepted and sent him her phone number.

NEW YORK CITY PUBLIC ADVOCATE, SALLIE ELKORDY'S OFFICE

Sallie watched her assistant, Natalie, hurrying towards her, with her pretty blonde, curly hair bouncing as she walked into her office. Sallie was sitting behind her desk going over plans for a Welcome Home Party for Brigitte. Sallie looked up and saw Natalie. "I have the perfect place in Times Square to throw this bash. Can you handle the event planning?"

Natalie with pen and paper in her hands took notes. "Yes, any particular color scheme or theme?"

Looking down at her notes, Sallie said, "Oldies, Old School, Throwback, whatever they are calling it nowadays. Lots of colors, like blues, greens, purples, maybe some red and gold, too. Terri is going to supply us with music."

While taking notes, Natalie looked up at Sallie. "Cool."

Sallie continued with her instructions. "I want to invite all Brigitte's social network friends and personal friends who supported her release. Brigitte's brother, wife, and Aunt Glo also. This is going to be awesome. So get those numbers for me. Terri and Brigitte will meet for the first time."

"I can't wait to meet Terri. I'll start making the calls," said Natalie.

LOS ANGELES

Marilyn and Terri were going over the non-profit documents and the pamphlet. Terri's smile lit up her whole face as she told Marilyn, "I can't thank you enough. Soon I will be able to help combat the raping of our children by sick and twisted people who think they have a God-given right to commit these atrocious crimes. The pamphlet I have created will help with questions such as: What is sexual abuse? Who commits these crimes? What are the signs of a molested child? We give the reasons why kids won't tell, and what we can do to get them to tell."

Marilyn asked, "Since you are not a licensed therapist, do you have hotlines for assistance?"

"Look on the back page. Yes, for children and if you are an adult still suffering psychologically from childhood sexual abuse. I will also have a hotline for the pedophiles and child molesters. They may want to get help or confess, you never know."

Marilyn looked at the pamphlet. "This looks great. I'm just curious. What is the difference between a child molester and a pedophile?"

Terri explained, "A child molester is a stranger to the victim and they usually kill them after molesting them. Pedophiles know their victims. They want the victim for constant sexual gratification so they groom them before the act. But, there are times they kill, out of fear of others finding out about their perversion. An Infantophile prefers children six and under. A Hebephile prefers a child at the cusp, and I mean the beginning of puberty, eleven to fourteen years of age. Then there's the Ephebophiles. They like kids who have reached puberty. Their ages are fifteen- to sixteen-year-olds."

Marilyn was looking at Terri as if she had seen a ghost and shocked at this bit of information.

"I know it's shocking, but there's the Teleiophile, they like seventeen-year-olds. I found information on all these different types of child sex crimes in an article, 'What is a Pedophile? Hebephile, Ephebophile, Teleiophile, Infantophile' in *Human Stupidity: Irrationality, Self-Deception,*' " said Terri.

"Wow. All I knew was a child molester. I guess there is a need to educate people about this. I have little ones in my family, and I would hate for them to have to endure this type of abuse. It's horrible," said Marilyn.

"Did you know that 80 percent of girls and 60 percent of boys are molested by family members and friends? Most abuse is by men and 20 percent of women rape boys. Thirty percent make up child molesters who were molested themselves. And, most in this group rarely try to inflict violent physical harm." I researched and found this information on the website in an article, 'Myths and Facts About Sex Offenders' – August 2000 and the site is www.csom.org/pubs/mythsfacts.html."

Marilyn still looked at Terri in amazement. "I am blown away. You have done your homework."

"Yes, and what's really horrible is not only the crime of the perpetrators, but the number of persons who allow it to hap-pen, and also the ones who won't believe the child because of the one who is being accused."

Terri suddenly held her head down and turned it from side to side. Marilyn noticed that Terri had changed from being happy to frowning, like she was almost ready to cry. Thinking about things from her past, Terri decided to open up to Marilyn.

"Just like Brigitte, my mother abandoned me when I was six months old. She asked her best friend to babysit me, so she could go out with Sam Cook. She never came back. I was told my father was part of the legendary "Mighty Clouds of Joy." When I turned nine, I went to live with him. He came to me with a Bible telling me the story of Adam and Eve, Lot, and Noah, and how all of them slept with family members. He was trying to convince me that incest was okay. Of course, when he saw I wasn't buying that, then came the threats. The reason I blame my mother is because she was not there to protect me. I think she knew he was sick. That's why she gave away all her girls. So, I went back to her best friend, and she raised me to be this woman I am today."

As she listened to her, Marilyn asked, "Did you ever tell your biological mother?"

Crying, Terri told her, "Yes, when I got older; and she didn't believe me. I even offered to tell her what his genitals looked like so she would believe me. She didn't want to hear it. She still doesn't. But the lady that raised me did. That's how I got through some of the pain."

Feeling her pain and hurt, Marilyn could only reach out to her and give her a hug, hoping it would make her feel a little better. After a few minutes, she looked at Terri and told her, "Now that we got that out, let's move on to a more positive subject. The party. Come on, get this ball rollin'. But I do suggest you get some counseling, Terri. It will help you be strong for the children out there who will need you to be, when they reach out to you."

Sitting back down in her chair, Terri looked off, knowing that Marilyn was right. Counseling would be good.

RHODE ISLAND

Tyson sat in his favorite comfy recliner chair, staring at the big screen TV and bookshelf. Two toy boxes for each child could be seen in the corner. Tyson seemed anxious. His wife, Sheena Harris, a beautiful Caucasian woman with pretty long curly hair, sat on the sofa with their two children, Michael and Melody. As she read books to them, she glanced over to her husband, who watched the wall clock. Sheena asked, "What's wrong, hon?"

"Terri hasn't called yet," said Tyson.

Looking at her husband, Sheena said, "She will. She always does."

"I know I..." Suddenly, his cell phone rang, and he answered it in a hurry. "Hello, Terri. I've been waiting for your call." He looked at Sheena, and she gave him a joyful smile. Terri gave them the update for the release party. Tyson answered, "Yes, we know where that is. It's in the New York Theater District." Sheena hurried and gave him a pen and paper.

Tyson wrote down all the information for the Welcome Home Party for his sister, Brigitte.

"Ok, let me repeat back to you. Nola Studio at 244 W. 54th St, 10th floor/studio #2 at 6 pm. Terri, thank you so much, and tell Sallie thanks also. We are so grateful for you. Thank you so much for all you've done for my sister," said Tyson.

Grabbing the children and whispering in their ears before Tyson hung up, they all said in unison, "Thank you, Terri!"

LOS ANGELES

It was thirty days before Brigitte's release, and Terri was at her wit's end, crying hysterically. She wanted to be at Brigitte's release from prison, but had no money. She knew that there was only one person she could turn to, so she got down on her knees.

"I'm sorry to sound like a big baby, but my heart is heavy. I'm just wondering, God, why can't I get to New York for Brigitte's release after all you've allowed me to do for her?" And right at that moment, her cell phone rang. She saw that it was Sallie and answered, "Hello." Terri knew that she must tell her that she would not be able to come to New York.

"Hello, Sallie. I won't be able to make it to the release party. I am livid right now. Can't afford the trip with all the other stuff I'm working on. Finances are tight." As she continued to listen to Sallie tell her it's okay and that she will proceed with everything for her, Terri answered with, "I know." Still listening to Sallie tell her not to cry or worry, she answered, "I sure will. Thank you so much. I owe you big time, Sallie. Bye now." Hanging up the phone, she knew that God answered prayers. She wiped her eyes, blew her nose and started to cry all over again.

Aware that prisons issued their own release outfits, Terri got up the next day and headed over to one of her favorite clothing department stores, Marshalls. Normally, the store is crowded, but on this particular day the flow of people was at a minimum. This made shopping and searching easier. Terri went through each rack slowly. She came across an outfit that brightened her eyes. It was a two-piece skirt outfit that was black and white with lace and had a cheetah print. Walking over to the shoe department, she also found a cute pair of ballerina shoes that matched perfectly with the outfit. Having only $30.00 in her purse, she checked the price of both items and walked up to the cashier.

The cashier ranged up both items and told her the total, "$27.99."

"Here you go."

"$2.01 is your change. Thank you for shopping here."

Terri knew her next goal was to get those clothes to Brigitte in time before her release. Feeling confident that this mission will be accomplished, she walked out of the store with a smile on her face. Terri went home and was able to make special arrangements for Brigitte to receive her clothing through one of the guards who offered to have Brigitte's clothes sent to her so she could get them to her in a timely manner.

NEW YORK

The big day, August 13, 2012, had finally arrived and Brigitte was scheduled to be released on parole.

Crowds of media, television vans setting up their satellites, camera people and news reporters scrambled and set up all over the front gate of the prison. Crowds of supporters had their signs up and shouted, "FREE-AT-LAST, FREE-AT-LAST, FREE-AT-LAST." Supporters were hyped up, excited, and the police were out for crowd control.

Waiting at the front of the gate was Tyson, Sheena, the kids, Aunt Glo, Sallie, Sallie's friends and Brigitte's friends. Processing the release of a prisoner took a few hours, and everyone was anxious for her release and on edge. And then suddenly, a guard swung the door open and out walked Brigitte dressed in her beautiful outfit and shaven head. She had a glow. Cameras were flashing as she walked towards the final gate. Her family and friends shouted her name while some cried tears of joy. Tyson and Aunt Glo could not wait for her to walk up to them. Instead, as Brigitte walked through the gate, they ran towards her with hugs and kisses. And then Sheena and Sallie had their turn. Brigitte looked down, saw her niece and nephew, grabbed them and hugged them tightly. The crowd continued to shout, "FREE-AT-LAST, FREE-AT-LAST, FREE-AT-LAST." People used their cell phones to record the moment, while reporters and cameramen clicked and snapped.

As they all headed over to the party, Brigitte used Tyson's phone and called Terri.

"Hello, Terri."

"BRIGITTE!" Terri screamed on the other end.

With tears streaming down her face, Brigitte told Terri. "I'm free, Terri. I wish you could have been here, but I am just glad I am free. We will see each other soon." Brigitte could hear Terri crying and apologizing for not being there. "Please don't cry. You're making me cry."

Terri asked if Debra was there. "No, Debra's not here, but I will enjoy the party without her. Thanks for helping Ms. Sallie Elkordy with the party. We're on our way there now. I am wearing the outfit you sent. Fits perfectly. I will send pictures. I did get the mail you sent about the non-profit, "Tell—Yell—Tell," for the sexually-abused kids. Just want to tell you the kids need you more than being here with me. So, know that. I know your heart, lady. Keep up the good work. You are a blessing to me. I will call you tomorrow."

After meeting so many of her supporters and friends, Brigitte was just overwhelmed, and happy. Now that the party was over, Brigitte was very tired. She and her family were staying in a hotel room with joining double doors. She liked knowing that her family was near and with her. Coming out of the bathroom, dressed in a pretty pink silk gown and slippers, she saw Tyson and Sheena were sitting on the bed talking. Aunt Glo, her niece and nephew were on the sofa bed and couch. Telling her family good night, she closed the adjoining door. Looking all around at her clean and decorated room, she gazed at the bed, as if she had never seen a bed in her whole life. She suddenly realized while slowly getting into bed who Lady Vengeance was talking about in her dream. The help that she was sending was Terri.

And then falling into a deep sleep, Brigitte saw Lady Vengeance running with haste to get out of the wicked dilapidated land of the pedophiles. With the help of the midnight blue skies lit up by the stars, she could see the edge of the land. She was dragging a huge cloak, filled with hundreds and hundreds of oyster shells. The waves of the roaring sea could be heard, beating up against the shores. Safety was near. Finally making it to the sea, she took her oyster-shell-handled golden staff and pointed it to the sea. As the sea spread apart, Lady Vengeance rushed through the parted waters, dragging her cloak through to the other side of the sea. And as she stepped upon the other side of the shore, she knew without a doubt that this new world was pure and free of wickedness. Taking her cloak, she twirled it round and round, watching the oyster shells fall out onto a sandy, blue shore. And then raising her staff, all the children of all ages came out of their shells laughing, playing and rejoicing.

LOS ANGELES

At LAX, jumping out of Marilyn's car dressed in a white suit, open toed high heel sandals, wearing bling, bling jewelry, and wearing her infamous braids, Terri rushed inside the airport, pulling her luggage behind her and checked in for her flight to New York. She was excited and happy knowing that she would finally meet Brigitte. They had both decided to do a book first before the release of the movie. So this would be an awesome time to have a Book Signing. And, it would be the first time they had ever met. It had been a long journey of ups and downs; but to her, it was well worth it. Sitting down and waiting patiently, she finally heard over the intercom from the announcer, "Now boarding flight 417 to New York, New York at gate 12."

Looking down at her ticket, she got up from her seat, grabbed her carry-on luggage and headed straight to the boarding entrance of the plane.

NEW YORK

Terri may have missed Brigitte's release but thanks to Sallie, working and saving her money she will finally meet Brigitte. Grabbing her luggage from the baggage area, she rushed outside and flagged down a cab. Giving instructions to the cabbie, he took her to Rockefeller Center and pulled up along the curb. Wanting to surprise Brigitte, she told her to meet her in front of the Tiffany Box. Getting out of the cab, she saw Tyson, Sheena, Aunt Glo and the kids. She also saw Sallie who suddenly turned around. Terri held her finger up to her mouth letting Sallie know to not say anything.

Brigitte, engrossed in conversation with Tyson, Sheena and Aunt Glo, did not see Terri. Terri walked up slowly to Brigitte and grabbed her hand. "Brigitte, I'm here." Brigitte, startled, turned around, jumped and saw that it was Terri. They each screamed, hugged and kissed each other on the cheek.

"Oh my God, Terri, finally, oh my God." Standing back and looking at each other, they gave each other a big hug.

Aunt Glo, waiting for her turn, stepped up and grabbed Terri's hand. "Okay, my turn, Terri. I have been waiting to thank you for everything you have done for Brigitte. I don't know where you came from, but thank God you're here."

Brigitte looked at both of them and said, "I know where she came from and who sent her, Auntie. One day I will tell you."

Aunt Glo grabbed Terri again hugging and kissing her on the cheek.

Tyson also stepped up with his wife, Sheena, and the kids. He told her, "Terri, I'm glad you made it. This is my wife Sheena and my children, Michael and Melody. We all have been dying to meet you."

Smiling and looking at Michael, Terri said, "I know. I felt I let everyone down when I couldn't make it for Brigitte's release, but I'm here now. It's on."

Sallie, looking at Terri, said, "Hi, lady. Much love," and then embraced her.

"Yes, much to you as well. As far as I'm concerned, you are all my new family 'cause we will be connected for life," said Terri.

Terri wanted a group picture and saw a stranger passing by. "Excuse me, sir. Can you take this picture for us?"

Smiling, the stranger said, "Sure, why not."

Everyone scrambled to pull themselves together for the group picture. The stranger grabbed the camera, focused on the group and told everyone to smile. Click. Handing the camera back to Terri, she told him, "Thank you so much." The stranger walked away, smiling.

Wanting to make this a night of festivities, Sallie made a suggestion. "Hey, why don't we go over to Trump Towers and catch a show?"

But Terri responded, "Nope. I'm making up for lost time and promises. I have two suites at the Waldorf Astoria. I've scheduled a dinner and show this evening."

And looking at Terri, Brigitte responded, "Ah, Terri, we have . . ."

Terri's finger came up, "Hold up, there's more, honey. Tomorrow, we go skating as we planned, Brigitte. I broke my promise not being at that gate when you were released. But, if God is willing, I will break no more promises."

Sheena immediately took out her cell phone to find a babysitter for the kids. Tyson and his wife flagged down a cab and took the children to the babysitter. Terri, Brigitte, Aunt Glo and Sallie caught a cab and went to the Waldorf Astoria Hotel. Terri checked in and they all waited for Tyson and Sheena to meet them there. Later on that evening and enjoying a nice dinner, they listened to the infamous 14-year-old Boy Bowers, a brilliant saxophone player. They all agreed that it was a most enjoyable evening.

NEW YORK – NEXT DAY

Meeting up at the ice skating rink located across from Rockefeller Center, Brigitte looked around at all the skaters and watched them laugh, talk and skate around the rink. She noticed her brother and his wife were affectionately skating around the rink. Sallie was on the sideline waving and smiling as she and Terri skated by her. Brigitte let out a sigh and thought, *"I believe I can finally move on now. I can now live and enjoy my life in peace and happiness with my family and friends. The memories will never go away, but I can do this."*

With Terri skating at her side, Brigitte told her, "Terri, this is so awesome. You didn't have to do all this."

"Yes, I did, Brigitte. You have helped me to unleash my demons that I have been battling for years. I've become a guardian angel now. Also, it's for all the children of the world and the hurting adults who need our help, Brigitte. Sallie is gonna give us all the guidance we need to get this message on the ballot and possibly change some laws as well as rallying our message state to state, bringing help and guidance to this dark subject no one wants to talk about. But we can't do it by ourselves either. We need the world to join our quest for it to be a success."

Embracing each other and then smiling, they both looked up and raised their hands towards Heaven in praise.

THE END

Humanitarians for Sexually Abused Children

MISSION STATEMENT

The mission of "TELL", is to inform the masses in an effort to increase reports, and punish those responsible for child sexual abuse. We will encourage children as well as adults to tell someone that an adult is, or has touched you no matter who it is. "TELL" will provide help for those crying out for help. Children are the future, and "TELL" is dedicated to ensuring that our future generations have a nurturing environment that will encourage them to grow into healthy adults.

How do we get the Kids to "TELL"

How Should I Respond? What Should I Say? These are commonly asked questions one of the most important things a parent can do is respond in a calm and matter-of-fact manner. Listen to the words and feelings of the child and observe his or her body language. Believe the child - children rarely lie about sexual abuse. If you don't have enough information about what is going on, it is a good idea to ask questions and let the child know you are someone they can safely talk to about this issue. Go to the doctor, have your child checked out. Be sure you do not ask accusing questions; such as; what were you doing to make them do that to you? The most important thing for you, as someone who cares about the child, is to say that no matter what happened or what they say, you will still love them. Also take the time to reassure the child that he or she has done nothing wrong. Let the child know that you will do whatever you can to keep him or her safe.

It is therefore important to Report Abuse and seek professional help and to not do this alone. There are resources throughout the country that can help a family through this difficult situation, See last page of Pamphlet for these organizations.

- Rape:
- Abuse:
- Incest: 1-800-656-HOPE (4673)
- National:
- Network:

National Child Sexual Abuse Helpline
1-866-FOR-LIGHT (367-5444)

Child Help USA National Child Abuse Hotline:
800-4-A-CHILD (422.4453)
800-2-A-CHILD (222.4453)

National Children's Alliance
(202) 548-0090 or (800) 239-9950

Parents for Megan's Law, the Crime Victim's Center for Support and Compensation 888-ask-pfml (888-275-7365) or 631-689-2672

Help TELL H.F.S.A.C. make a difference! H.F.S.A.C. would like to build safe havens for abused children. If you would like to make a donation, please go to:

www.culturedpearlsentertainment.com

TERRI JOHNSON

BRIGITTE HARRIS